D1738622

How To Stop Being A Narcissist

Complete Guide On How To Give Up Control In Relationships

How To Recognize And Stop Controlling Narcissistic Behavior

Antony Felix

Introduction

Even if you have not read Publius Ovidius Naso's (Ovid) magnum opus, Metamorphoses in its entirety, you have heard of the story of Narcissus, right? If you haven't, the legend goes like this:

One day, Narcissus, a Laconian hunter who was the son of the nymph Liriope and the river god Cephissus, was walking through the woods.

Echo, an Orestiad (Oread) or mountain nymph, saw him, fell in love with his beauty, and started following him. At the time, after suspecting Echo of consorting with her husband Zeus, Hera had cursed the nymph: she could only speak the last words spoken to her.

As Ovid notes in book 3 of Metamorphoses, after suspecting that someone was following him, Narcissus called out. Echo, now so enthralled with Narcissus, gave caution to the wind (and her curse), revealed herself, then tried to embrace him. Narcissus would have none of that. He told her to leave him alone.

Heartbroken and dejected, Echo spent the rest of her life lonely, repeating the last words she heard Narcissus say, "farewell." The words eventually became a faint echo, and

Echo wasted away. Nemesis, the goddess of revenge, learned of the story and decided to punish Narcissus.

Later, after a long summer day of hunting, Narcissus felt thirsty. As mythology has it, the goddess of revenge used this opportunity to lure him to a pool of water. Upon looking into the water, Narcissus saw his reflected beauty and fell deeply in love with himself. He became immensely obsessed with himself, but because his reflection could not reciprocate the love he felt for it, he wasted away.

Learn more:

https://bit.ly/3bMM6dZ

Whether this narrative happened or is pure mythology does not matter. It is, however, relevant because the term narcissism comes from the character traits displayed by Narcissus after he fell in love with himself.

Dictionary.com defines narcissism as an "excessive interest in or admiration of oneself and one's physical appearance."

Self-admiration is not a crime. Neither is a healthy level of self-importance or self-esteem and self-confidence. However, when both tether on a vain sense of self, narcissism is the resultant character.

According to psychology[1], Narcissistic Personality Disorder (NDP) is one of the three dark triads; the other two are psychopathy and Machiavellianism.

Some key characteristics of the disorder are a deeply-rooted sense of self-importance, a lack of empathy, and an unhealthy need for admiration. Other character traits related to NDP include an obsessive focus on [one's] physical appearance, taking advantage of others, and an obsession with success and power, among many others.

In this guide, we shall seek to cultivate a deeper understanding of narcissism. Above that, we shall discuss various steps and strategies that can help you recognize and stop narcissistic or controlling behavior.

Let's get started!

---

[1] https://www.sciencedirect.com/topics/psychology/dark-triad#:~:text=The%20Dark%20Triad%20(DT)%20is,Paulhus%20%26%20Williams%2C%202002).&text=Though%20DT%20research%20focuses%20on,its%20own%20independent%20literature%20base.

PS: I'd like your feedback. If you are happy with this book, please leave a review on Amazon.

Please leave a review for this book on Amazon by visiting the page below:

https://amzn.to/2VMR5qr

Table of Contents

Part I

Understanding Narcissism

This book has been divided into parts, so let's begin with Part 1, which helps you understand narcissism, a complex and often misunderstood personality trait and disorder. Here, we will find out what narcissism truly entails by breaking down its characteristics and various forms. After that, we will learn how to recognize narcissistic behavior to help you identify it in yourself and others. Lastly, we will look at the causes of Narcissistic Personality Disorder (NPD), exploring the psychological, environmental, and genetic factors that contribute to its development.

This part sets the foundation for dealing with narcissist traits because it allows you to understand the roots and signs of narcissism, giving you a deeper understanding of this unhealthy behavior and setting the stage for exploring its impacts and how to manage it effectively.

Chapter 1: A Deeper Look At Narcissism

To ensure you have a firmer idea of what narcissism is, the first thing we need to do is define it better.

The Mayo Clinic states:

"Narcissistic Personality disorder (NCP) is a mental disorder or condition where the afflicted experience an inflated sense of personal importance. Narcissistic people have a deeply seated desire for attention, admiration, and validation, and are often non-empathetic towards others."

Worth noting here is that from this definition, being a narcissist sounds a lot like what we call *"being full of yourself,"* which, common terminology notwithstanding, translates to self-obsession.

Narcissism has elements of self-assuredness, yes, but these elements often become so pronounced that they teeter on self-centeredness. However, in itself, a certain degree of being self-centered is not unhealthy or a personality disorder.

Doubtlessly, and as many mental health experts have stated, a healthy degree of self-centeredness is essential for your mental health. Roger Gil, a mental health expert, for example, notes that there is a difference between clinical narcissism (NDP) and loving the sound of your voice or being self-centered. To some degree, the latter is healthy.

That should also tell you that the line between narcissism (NCP) and healthy self-confidence (and a healthy sense of self) is very slim.

The primary difference between the two is that a confident person has a healthy sense of self —what we call an affirmative sense of self-esteem. This healthy, non-clouded sense of self ensures that the ego of a confident person remains in check and that they are capable of considering the feelings and needs of others.

For the narcissistic, the ego, as well as the unhealthy, grandiose sense of self, know no limitations. Narcissists see no fault in their personalities. Even when a narcissist is the most 'self-deficient' person in the room, they will have a clouded sense of self. The ego and sense of self of a narcissist become so inflated that everything becomes about him or her.

Narcissists always find a way to focus the conversation on themselves and their achievement, superiority, or 'specialness' compared to 'other humans.' For instance, instead of asking your partner questions that help create a bond, if you are a narcissist, you are likely to seek attention by rerouting the conversation to yourself.

In their extreme, ego, self-importance, and self-centeredness can ruin relationships.

An example that illustrates this is the disability to take constructive criticism. Narcissists have a very fragile sense of confidence built on external affirmation. Because of this, they are unable to take criticism or responsibility. Instead, they shift blame, and as you know, shifting blame is usually a cause of relationship strife.

Another vital thing worth noting is that, unlike healthy self-confidence, clinical or pathological narcissism is a personality impairment. That is why we call it Narcissistic Personality Disorder (NDP). Because it is a personality disorder, narcissists do not have a healthy view of themselves. It's also why most of them cannot relate to others or exercise empathy.

Further, because it creates a fragile sense of self-esteem that's dependent on constant validation and affirmation, narcissistic behaviors and tendencies are unhealthy in the following sense.

Thanks in part to the fragile nature of a narcissist's ego, most narcissists tend to embellish their skills, achievements, or 'specialness.' Often, the desire to do this is out of a need to receive validation or admiration. Because of this need and desire, most narcissists cannibalize relationships. They also monopolize conversations. Because of the desire to keep everything centered on them, most narcissists are very impatient to the point of being disdainful towards those trying to take attention away from them.

Further, pathological narcissists often react angrily —or negatively— to anything that hurts their fragile ego and self-esteem. For instance, narcissists overreact to any opinion that misaligns with their self-perception. Such a person may, for example, react with unjustified anger towards any criticism. In most cases, however, narcissists react with deliberation and calculation, often driven by the desire to protect the fragile ego and 'feel special.'

Up to this point, we have discussed everything you need to know to understand narcissism more deeply. With this knowledge, we can start discussing how to recognize narcissistic behavior in yourself and others:

How To Recognize Narcissistic Behavior

To recognize narcissistic behavior in yourself and others, the first thing you need to realize is that, as mentioned earlier, narcissism occurs in degrees.

First, there is an *adaptive level of narcissism*. This level of narcissism is healthy; it, therefore, does not cause narcissistic personality disorder. Adaptive narcissism helps you believe in yourself, be confident, and practice self-care as part of your wellbeing routine.

Then, there's *maladaptive narcissism*, which occurs in varying degrees, too. In this guide, we shall concentrate on learning how to recognize pathological narcissism (NDP). When experienced at a pathological level, narcissism can interfere with your relationships, happiness, and general wellbeing.

In essence, what we shall discuss are the various signs and symptoms of pathological narcissism.

NOTE: It's paramount to mention that assessment by a mental health expert is the best way to recognize and diagnose clinical narcissism.

That notwithstanding, if you notice many of the following tendencies or behaviors in yourself —and in someone close to you— seek a professional opinion with some degree of immediacy:

You Love Your Reflection A Bit Too Much

We talked about Narcissus and how, after catching a glimpse of his reflection, he fell in love with it so much that he could not look away. He ended up wasting away in front of a pool of water —some narratives say that he drowned. We mentioned the relevance of the narrative to NDP by stating that it's from here that we get the original definition of the term narcissism.

If your mirror reflection enthralls you so much that you can't pass a mirror without stopping to admire and marvel at your beauty, this could count as narcissistic behavior.

It's worth mentioning here that there's nothing wrong with admiring yourself or spending a moment in front of a mirror, working to make sure your outward image is 'in place.' The kind of self-enthrallment we are talking about here is the maladaptive kind that leads to an obsession with your self-image. This kind of obsession breeds an unhealthy self-image and belief system.

Grandiosity

Grandiosity is one of the hallmark traits of pathological narcissism. It often reflects as having an unhealthy sense of self-importance that is pretentious and, therefore, lacking a basis in reality. The level of grandiosity in question here is the unrealistic kind that surpasses a healthy level of confidence to the point of being arrogant and vain.

If your personality is narcissistic, you will believe that you have an extra layer of 'special' that no one can match or surpass. You are also likely to believe that because you are 'special,' associating with those 'beneath you' is, well, beneath you. Because of this belief, you will go out of your way to associate with those you think are your peers. Most of the time, these will be high-status people, things, and places.

Because of an inflated sense of grandiosity, above believing you are the 'best' or better than everyone, you are also likely to expect others to treat you accordingly. For instance, even when you have done nothing worthwhile, you will likely expect others to admire or treat you with reverence. This desire for recognition will also likely drive you into embellishing your capabilities and achievements —if not lying about them.

Further, out of a need to ensure that others treat you with admiration, every conversation you have is likely to cycle back to how amazing you are. For instance, when talking about work projects, you will concentrate on highlighting how much you contributed to the success of an endeavor. You will not feel compelled to mention the contributions made by others. The primary driver of all this is a need to illustrate your 'amazingness' so that others, even loved ones, can treat you like a star —and feel special to have you in their lives.

Shifting Blame —Even When You Are At Fault

Shifting blame —even when you are at fault— is another characteristic you can use to recognize narcissistic behavior in yourself (and others).

As previously mentioned, narcissists react angrily (overly so) to criticism of any kind because it contradicts their 'glorified' ego and false self-image. Because of this, they offend easily, especially in relationships.

Above that, if you are a narcissist, in the face of criticism or an opinion that contradicts your false self-image, you will shift blame or attack the person voicing the opinion/criticism. For instance, if your partner talks to you about how neglected they feel, you are likely to shift this blame, perhaps by outlining how much you are doing for them.

Shifting blame —even when you are at fault —makes it impossible to practice self-criticism, which, on its part, makes practicing self-growth a challenge.

An obvious issue that comes with shifting blame is not accepting responsibility. When you cannot accept responsibility for your actions and behaviors, it strains your personal and work relationships. Success in these areas of your life demands that you be open to growth, which can only happen when you are self-critical and ready to accept your responsibilities.

When you cannot accept your shortcomings or faults, no one will want to collaborate or be with you in a committed relationship. Moreover, ignoring feedback from your loved ones will likely leave them feeling unheard and neglected, which will strain your relationships further.

Your Obsession With Your Outer Image Knows No Bounds

A rabid obsession with your image is a behavior commonly found in narcissistic individuals. It's not too farfetched to imagine that if Narcissus lived in the modern age, his obsessions with his outer image would have no equal. As it is, he became so obsessed with his outer beauty that he could not stop staring at it —he died looking at a reflection of his face.

If you have a narcissistic personality, practicing a modicum of self-awareness will reveal that you spend a lot of money on self-grooming. Sometimes more than you can afford. You spend this money because you want to look as if you have a higher social standing. Another thing you will notice is that you spend a lot of time and energy on personal grooming.

A study conducted in 2008 by Simine Vazire et al. showed that it was relatively easy for an atypical observer to recognize someone with narcissistic tendencies. They revealed that narcissistic people have specific dressing, makeup, and jewelry choices. For example, they are likely to favor brand clothes and accouterments.

In particular, the researchers showed that narcissistic men are likely to have a flashy sense of fashion. Women, on the other hand, are likelier to show an excessive amount of cleavage and wear 'loud' makeup.

These findings are congruent with everything we have discussed thus far about narcissistic behavior. If you have narcissistic tendencies, out of an obsession with appearing 'high-status,' your fashion choices are likely to reflect this because you want others to notice and recognize you.

You Favor A Shift-Response Over A Support-Response

A shift-response is a conversational approach that shifts the focus away from your conversation partner and on to yourself. A support response, on the other hand, uses prompting to keep the conversation on the other person.

Take an example where you are in a conversation with person A. As a narcissist, when person A says, *"I want to buy a phone,"* you will not prompt them with questions. You are unlikely to say, *"Yeah? Do you have a brand or name in mind?"*

Instead, you will shift the conversation to the Samsung Galaxy S20 Ultra you bought. You will talk about how amazing it is, how much it cost you, and how 'rich' you have to be to afford it. This conversational approach is one of the hallmark traits of narcissism. If you notice such a tendency in yourself, pay more attention and seek a medical diagnosis.

When you adopt a shift-response, every interaction becomes driven by the desire to focus on yourself so that you can use the opportunity to show how unique or remarkable you are. Instead of listening to hear and understand what others communicate and using this to drive forth a connection, you listen for cues to shift the conversation to you.

To notice if you favor the shift-response, pay attention to your conversational interactions with loved ones and colleagues. If you cannot go five minutes without wondering when a conversation will get back to you" or actively shifting attention to yourself, you have narcissistic tendencies.

You Live In A Fantasy World

Narcissists are never as incredible as they make themselves out to be —or believe they are. In most cases, they have self-esteem issues. Because of this, they tend to live in a fantasy-driven mental world where they can reconcile their delusions of grandeur with the reality of their lives, which is that they are imperfect!

If you often spin a good tale about how fabulous, rich, successful, handsome, or beautiful you are —even though you are none of these things— these are narcissistic tendencies. If you often glorify and embellish your brilliance, success, power, beauty, or attractiveness, you have created a fantasy world where these things are real. This realization should stir you into seeking a professional diagnosis.

Narcissists usually create a fantasy world as a way to protect a fragile ego and to receive the external validation and affirmation they crave because they feel internally inadequate. If you are a narcissist, your courtship with this fantasy world is why you react angrily to opinions and criticism that threaten your fragile self-perception.

You Crave Admiration and Praise

Narcissists have a very fragile ego that deflates in the absence of admiration, recognition, and praise. That is why if you are a narcissist, you are likely to seek more than genuine compliments from your partner. Instead, because your fragile ego and self-image depend on it, you will likely want your partner or colleagues to provide you with a constant stream of affirmations.

As discussed, narcissists have an aversion to criticism and dissenting opinions, especially those that contradict the fantasy world they have created. Because of this indifference, their best company is made up of YES men and women, who are liberal with compliments and praise.

When any of the YES men or women around you become unforthcoming with praise and compliments, you treat it as a betrayal and react accordingly. Often, this reaction is angry or manipulative, aimed at getting the person to offer what you want: *affirmation*!

Lack of Empathy

A lack of empathy is another trait commonly displayed by those who have narcissistic tendencies. Empathy is the ability to understand and relate to where other people are coming from, what they are feeling, and their opinions. Narcissists lack this ability.

Instead, if you are a narcissist, your primary concern shall always be your needs and what you can do to fulfill them. The lack of empathy, your driving need to get your way all the time, and the self-centeredness they breed make having good relationships a challenge.

Because a narcissist cannot relate to what other people feel, when you are one, you never hesitate to exploit others to achieve a desirable end. Your primary concern shall be getting what you want (your way). Because of this, you will treat the special people in your life like pieces you can manipulate on a chessboard.

Additionally, because you will feel superior and deserving of admiration, you will usually be oblivious to the harmful effects your words and actions have on others. Instead, in part because of a lack of empathy, you will often believe that others are lucky for the chance to help you get what you want and to be in your life. This belief will strain your relations with those you exploit maliciously or out of the [oblivious] delusion that you are worship-worthy.

If you are a narcissist, in addition to being self-absorbed, you are also likely to want to control everything (be a control freak). That also means you will become desolate or blame others when things fail to work out as you wish. Moreover, because you shall be intolerant to contradicting views and apathetic to the emotional and psychological needs of others, things failing to go your way shall lead to angry outbursts.

If you are a narcissist, to protect your fantasy world and self-image, you will often resort to using underhanded strategies to get your way. For instance, in the face of criticism or opinions that contradict your "I'm special" self-image, you may devalue, derogate, or even insult the person voicing that criticism or opinion.

Self-Reflection

Here is a worksheet to help you reflect and get a better understanding of what we have discovered so far:

Question 1: Describe how you would have defined narcissism before reading this chapter:

_____

_____

_____

_____

Question 2: Describe your understanding of narcissism from this chapter:

_____

_____

_____

_____

Question 3: Would you say that you have healthy or unhealthy self-confidence?

_____

_____

Question 4: Do you tend to blame others or your circumstances for unfavorable outcomes in different situations, or do you value and practice accountability?

_____

_____

_____

Question 5: True or False? Narcissists are able to take responsibility for their actions and accept blame easily.

_____

_____

Question 6: Do your relationships last long, and can you say that the other person is genuinely happy, satisfied, and looking forward to a future with you?

_____

_____

_____

Question 7: When someone criticizes you, do you:

A. Accept the feedback and consider it.

B. Get defensive and shift the blame.

C. Ignore it completely.

Question 8: Do you feel the need to always highlight your achievements in conversations?

A. Yes, I often bring up my successes.

B. Sometimes, if it's relevant.

C. No, I focus on the topic at hand.

And,

In social settings, do you:

A. Listen and respond to others' stories.

B. Quickly shift the conversation to your experiences.

C. Mostly stay silent.

Question 9: Based on your responses, do you recognize any narcissistic tendencies in yourself?

_____

_____

_____

(Note: Reflect honestly on your answers and consider if they indicate narcissistic behavior.)

To recognize if you display narcissistic behavior, use the guidelines we have outlined here to evaluate yourself as honestly as possible. If you notice a large number of these behaviors and character traits in your personality, you are likely a narcissist or have NPD.

Moving on to the second chapter, let us discuss what causes this personality trait/disorder.

Chapter 2: Causes of Narcissistic Personality Disorder

As is usually the case with personality disorders, the scientific community has not yet reached a consensus or pinpointed the exact cause of narcissistic personality (NDP) disorder. Many experts, however, believe its primary causes to be a combination of psychological factors, early childhood experiences, and genes.

Examples of early childhood experiences related to the development of NDP include early childhood trauma and parenting models. As an example, experts have noted that when parents pamper a child or [overly] concentrate on a child's appearance or talent, it can cause personality issues such as narcissism.

Parental neglect, over-criticism, trauma or abuse, and high expectations are the other factors that can predispose a child to personality disorders such as NDP.

In this chapter, we shall discuss some of NDP's causative factors in more detail. By doing this, you should have a deeper understanding of what causes narcissism:

Resistance To Vulnerability

Seth Meyers Psy.D., a licensed clinical psychologist, notes that a firm resistance to vulnerability is one of the root causes of narcissism.

As he explains it, narcissism is a result of resistance to vulnerability because even when in a relationship, out of a desire to appear perfect, a narcissistically inclined person is unable to trust others. This disability, or rather, disinclination, to trust others is usually because the narcissist is afraid that a close look will reveal personality deficiencies.

Meyers further notes that narcissism develops when someone cannot —or chooses not to— trust others because doing so requires a degree of vulnerability. Since vulnerability does not sit well with the fake self-image that is so common among narcissists, most of them are unwilling to do it. Instead, they remain hypervigilant against anything they consider a threat to the self-superiority they have created in their minds.

Narcissism usually develops out of a desire to protect a false internal and external self-image driven by fear —more so the fear of 'being found wanting.' To protect this fragile self-image, the narcissistic-ly inclined keep others at bay, lest they learn something that they can use to gain power over the narcissist.

Additionally, to maintain a sense of superiority —albeit a false one— that keeps vulnerability at bay, most narcissists develop a tendency to overcompensate and over-embellish. For instance, when someone who is narcissistic-ly predisposed feels weak and vulnerable, they are likely to act out in anger. If not, such a person is likely to act in a manner that helps them feel in control, even if doing so ends up hurting others.

From his clinical practice, Dr. Seth Meyers discovered that narcissism develops because of a need to protect a false and fragile self-image and ego. He further notes that when someone who is narcissistic-ly inclined experiences something that breeds a sense of inferiority, they create a grandiose, false self-image. The person then uses this false sense of self-esteem to prop up the ego and feel better.

Dr. Meyers concludes that pathological narcissism develops when, instead of introspecting and engaging in self-reflection, someone who is feeling 'deficient' creates a false, narcissistic inner persona. As he notes, this false persona helps the narcissistic individual avoid feeling the brunt of the vulnerability and uncertainty that comes with feeling inadequate or wanting on a personal level.

Narcissistic Wound And Indulgence

Preston Ni, a professor of communications at Foothill College, Silicon Valley, California, is a thought leader in the field of communication and narcissism. He notes that two primary pathologies, narcissistic wound and narcissistic indulgence, are the primary causes of narcissism:

Narcissistic Wound

Like Dr. Meyers, Preston Ni believes that narcissism develops when someone who is narcissistically inclined experiences 'something' that leaves them feeling inadequate. To compensate for the wound caused by not feeling good enough —what Professor Ni calls a narcissistic wound— the person creates a false self that masks the vulnerability.

He notes that most narcissistic wounds trace back to challenging, early childhood experiences of a familial or social nature. The professor further mentions that when someone whose self-esteem is fragile experiences societal pressure and familial conflict in early childhood, the result is narcissistic behavior.

For example, after a narcissistic wound leaves a narcissistically inclined person feeling humiliated, hurt, or inadequate, the person creates a false persona that helps them feel adequate, worthy, or loved.

Professor Ni adds that narcissistic wounds are the cause of narcissism because their occurrence is what causes a narcissistically inclined person to adopt compensatory schemes. Instead of developing resiliency skills, the person creates an alter ego, a false sense of self, grandiosity, and other character traits associated with narcissism.

Unfortunately, as noted by Professor Ni and other mental health professionals, the creation of this alter ego is of very little help, which is why narcissists have fragile personalities. This fragility and an ongoing sense of personal inadequacy fuels continued narcissistic behavior.

Narcissistic Indulgence

Like narcissistic wounds, Professor Ni notes that narcissistic indulgence also develops in early childhood. Narcissistic indulgences are instances where those around someone with fragile self-esteem engage in behaviors that lead the person to believe that they are 'special' or 'better than.'

As an example, when parents and family members overindulge a child's whims and make them feel 'incapable of doing any wrong,' a narcissistic personality is the most likely resultant character trait.

Like Professor Ni, most mental health experts agree that early childhood overindulgences are one of the primary causes of narcissistic tendencies, especially in young adults.

That consensus makes sense because when familial, social, and societal conditions lead a moldable child to believe they are superior or deserve special treatment, this can lead to an inflated ego.

While many of these experts also agree that there's nothing wrong with praising a child, they also note that under criticism and letting a child get away with anything is unhealthy because it breeds a sense of entitlement, a character trait commonly displayed by most narcissists.

When [whatever] circumstances lead a child into believing that they are the exception to the rule, an exceptional, one-of-a-kind person who deserves uncommon privileges, it acts as fodder for the formation of indulgent, narcissistic behaviors. It also causes the child in question to believe that they can use and mistreat others without any repercussion; after all, 'superior' beings can do what they want and get away with it, can't they?

When a child adopts such a belief system, they feel entitled to indulgence, which leads to indulgent, narcissistic behaviors (indulgent narcissism). Believing that 'walking on air' or 'being pedestalized' is a birthright, such a child considers him or herself the center of the world.

Because of this, as Professor Ni notes, such a child is likely to develop a narcissistic shell. Although externally arrogant-seeming, this shell acts as a shield for a self-image that is too fragile to survive without external validation.

Based on his work, Professor Ni believes that narcissistic wounds and narcissistic indulgences are the primary factors that cause otherwise healthy people to develop tendencies. He notes that these two facts are the primary cause of the self-absorption, lack of empathy, manipulation, and the other character traits attached to narcissistic personality disorder.

#: Parental Inconsistencies (And Approach)

The consensus amongst mental health experts is the childhood stage is very defining, enough to determine the kind of character and belief system someone adopts. Many experts believe using the wrong parenting approaches and strategies during this critical phase of development can cause the development of a narcissistic personality.

In particular, many health experts agree that parental inconsistencies are a primary cause of NDP. For instance, a lack of congruency between what parents say and do can lead to confusion that causes a child to develop personality issues such as NDP.

Most experts also believe that inconsistent parenting approaches that make it challenging for a child to determine how a parent will react (or act) to a circumstance can lead to insecurities, low self-esteem, or the development of a narcissistic, false shelf/self.

A common type of parental inconsistency manifests as instances where parents who feel incapable or deficient shower their children with exaggerated, empty praise and rewards or go overboard with criticism. As a response, the children of such parents develop a deeply-seated, false sense of self that helps them cope with and manage the environment.

For many years, psychiatrists believed that the primary cause of narcissism was a lack of love and affection in the home environment. Today, however, many in this community believe that parental overcompensation and failure to teach children coping strategies can contribute to this.

Additionally, most experts believe that narcissism in early childhood does not necessarily translate into narcissism in young adulthood and later. Most psychiatrists believe that a degree of narcissistic behavior is normal in young children, especially in the sense that children are likely to treat small milestones as major ones.

To help guard against the transitional development of narcissistic behavior from childhood to adolescence and adulthood, mental health experts advise parents to indulge in age-appropriate narcissism but also teach children healthy coping skills, especially in the face of failure and setbacks.

Having discussed narcissism deeply, its core characteristics, and known causes, we can move on to discussing how to manage it.

Before we do that, it is worth mentioning that narcissism is more common, especially in men, than most people assume or believe. In 2008, the Journal of Clinical Psychiatry published a study showing that 6.2 of the population is likely to be narcissistic.

Another study published in 2018 in the journal PLOS One noted that we are living in a society where narcissism is on the rise, especially in Western societies. Vater A, Moritz S, and Roepke S, the authors of the study, went as far as to say that our societies are experiencing a 'narcissism epidemic.'

If engaging in self-inventory reveals that you have narcissistic tendencies that are straining your relationships, causing you to engage in self-harming behaviors and addictions, take heart. If you are committed to self-betterment, you can do something about bettering yourself. You can also learn how to stop practicing controlling, narcissistic behavior and give up control in relationships.

Self-Reflection

Question 1: What can you say led to your Narcissistic behaviors or traits? Could you say it was psychological factors, early childhood experiences, genes, genetic predisposition, social influences, or peer pressure?

_____

_____

Question 2: Describe some of your childhood experiences that could be associated with the development of narcissism:

_____

_____

_____

_____

Question 3: Do you let yourself be vulnerable? If not, do you think that your resistance to vulnerability contributes to your narcissism?

_____

_____

_____

_____

(Note: Reflect on whether your inability to trust others is due to a fear that vulnerability will expose your perceived deficiencies.)

Question 4: Do you create a false self-image to maintain a sense of superiority? And, in what ways do you overcompensate to protect your self-image?

_____

_____

_____

_____

(Note: Think about if you act out in anger or adopt controlling behaviors to feel in control and superior, even if it harms others.)

Question 5: Have you experienced a narcissistic wound, according to Preston Ni?

_____

_____

_____

_____

(Note: Reflect on whether you have encountered situations that made you feel inadequate, leading you to create a false self to mask your vulnerability.)

Question 6: Can you provide an example of how a narcissistic wound developed in your early childhood?

_____

_____

_____

_____

(Note: Consider if familial conflict or societal pressure made you feel humiliated or inadequate, prompting you to create a grandiose persona to feel worthy and loved.)

Question 7: Have you experienced narcissistic indulgence, and how did it develop in your life?

_____

_____

_____

_____

_____

___

(Note: Think back to see if you were overindulged as a child and led to believe you were special or superior, resulting in an inflated ego and a sense of entitlement.)

Question 8: How have your parents' or guardians' inconsistencies in your upbringing contributed to the development of narcissist traits?

_____

_____

_____

_____

(Note: Reflect on whether inconsistent parenting, such as a mismatch between actions and words, confused you and led to insecurities or the development of a false self to cope with your environment.)

Question 9: What behaviors exhibited by your parents might have contributed to your narcissism?

_____

_____

_____

_____

*(**Note**: Reflect on if your parents over-praised you without criticism, provided empty rewards, or were overly critical.*

Question 10: Why is it crucial for you to learn healthy coping skills and overcome narcissism, according to mental health experts?

_____

_____

_____

_____

*(**Note:** Base your answers on what you have learned so far in this book or from other resources.)*

With this knowledge, let's get to the second part.

Part II

Understanding the Impact of Narcissism on Relationships

This part builds up your understanding of narcissism by covering the impacts of this trait on your relationships. We are social beings, and relationships, whether personal or professional, are important in our lives. However, these narcissistic behaviors negatively affect your relationships, making your life harder than it should be and hindering growth, happiness, and fulfillment.

Let's get right into it and discover how being a narcissist affects your personal and professional life. This will give you a clue of how important it is to commit to the effective strategies we will discuss later.

Chapter 3: Understanding the Impact of Narcissism on Your Relationships

You have probably been wondering why you seem to be on bad terms with everyone or have too many issues in your personal and professional relationships. Well, here is your answer: According to E.B. Johnson[2], a NLPMP coach, having narcissistic traits makes it almost impossible to have healthy relationships. Mainly, this is because you are unable to be empathetic with others and are always in need of validation, among other behaviors we discussed earlier, which may hurt your relationships and cause devastating damage to your victims, some of who never recover.

Here is an example of just how unspeakable the damage can be. According to studies[3], children brought up by narcissistic parents tend to have brain damage due to maltreatment and psychological abuse. This damage can have many negative impacts on the children's lives, which they walk with into

[2]   https://medium.com/practical-growth/this-is-the-real-reason-narcissists-struggle-to-form-healthy-relationships-b1b4932b707a

[3]   https://www.healthline.com/health/mental-health/children-of-narcissistic-parents#:~:text=A%202012%20study%20suggested%20that,traumatic%20stress%20disorder%20(PSTD).

their teenage years and adulthood if not addressed. The impacts are the same for adults, especially in marriages, friendships, work relationships, and family dynamics.

In this chapter, we will cover the impacts of narcissism and NPD on your romantic and professional relationships.

Effects of Narcissism on Intimate Relationships

Most of us display classic narcissistic symptoms from time to time, which has affected society as a whole. However, these tendencies or behaviors are more invasive in romantic relationships and have been found to leave many couples unhappy[4]. These feelings of unhappiness are likely to be accompanied by several negative effects, such as:

Erosion of Trust and Emotional Intimacy

As a narcissist, you might find it challenging to cultivate genuine emotional intimacy. Your need for constant admiration and validation can often overshadow your

---

4

https://uknowledge.uky.edu/cgi/viewcontent.cgi?article=1058&context=kaleidoscope#:~:text=The%20current%20study%20was%20able,more%20frequent%20and%20severe%20conflict.

partner's needs, leading to several detrimental behaviors that erode trust and emotional closeness.

These behaviors include:

- *Lack of Empathy*: One of the main characteristics of narcissism is a lack of empathy, and without it, it becomes difficult for you to understand or value your partner's feelings and needs. As a result, you might emotionally neglect your partner, leaving them feeling isolated and unimportant. In turn, this neglect can damage the emotional bond between you.

- *Manipulation and Control:* You may use manipulative tactics to control your partner, creating an unbalanced power dynamic. Manipulation and controlling behaviors include gaslighting and emotional blackmail, among others, and they leave your partner feeling powerless and unsure of themselves. As a result, trust wears thin, leaving your relationship in a world of fear and uncertainty.

- *Inconsistency and Unpredictability:* Your behavior might be inconsistent, swinging between idealizing and devaluing your partner. One moment, you may shower them with affection, and the next, criticize or belittle them. Being unpredictable and inconsistent makes it hard for your partner to feel secure in the relationship, leading to constant anxiety and doubt.

Communication and Conflict Resolution Challenges

Some of your traits can make it hard for you to employ healthy conflict resolution methods and have open and honest communication in your relationship with your partner, and recognizing these behaviors is the first step toward improvement.

The culprit traits that make it hard for you and your partner to communicate and address conflicts effectively include:

- *Defensiveness and Blame-Shifting*: You might find yourself becoming highly defensive and unwilling to accept responsibility for your actions. Instead of acknowledging your role in conflicts, you may shift the blame onto your partner. And in as much as you might want this unhealthy behavior to work, it escalates situations and prevents you from finding solutions, leaving issues unresolved and festering.

- *Intolerance to Criticism:* Any form of criticism, even if constructive, might trigger your narcissistic rage or cause you to withdraw. This hypersensitivity to perceived slights can make honest and open communication difficult.

- *Lack of Constructive Communication*: You may struggle with effective communication, often dominating conversations, interrupting, or dismissing your partner's viewpoints. This tendency to control the dialogue can lead to frustration and make your partner feel unheard and unvalued.

Dependency and Isolation

Even if you try your best not to display narcissistic traits to your partner, sometimes, you might be unable to help yourself. With time, your partners can become emotionally dependent[5] on your approval and validation, creating unhealthy dynamics in your relationships.

For example, your partner is likely to:

- *Become Codependent:* Your partner may develop codependent tendencies, where their sense of self-worth becomes tied to your approval. This unhealthy bond makes it hard for them to leave the relationship, even if it becomes toxic.

- *Become Socially Isolated:* You might isolate your partner from their friends and family to increase your control and

---

5   https://www.drgeorgesimon.com/why-narcissists-attract-the-emotionally-dependent/

their dependency on you. This behavior can leave your partner feeling trapped and unsupported, as they lose their external support network.

Emotional Abuse and Gaslighting

Some of your behaviors might be emotionally abusive to your partner, severely affecting the growth and progress of your relationship.

The main behaviors are:

- *Gaslighting:* You may find yourself persistently denying facts or feelings that are important to your partner, leading to confusion and self-doubt. This manipulation causes your partner to distrust their own reality and you. However, you need to recognize your partner's emotions and experiences and emotions without dismissing them to promote trust and understanding.

- *Devaluation:* Over time, you might devalue your partner through constant criticism, insults, and belittling comments. This behavior can destroy your partner's self-esteem and sense of worth, making emotional closeness impossible.

Infidelity and Betrayal

Your constant need for admiration and validation might lead you to engage in infidelity[6] or other forms of betrayal.

How?

- *Cheating:* You may seek out other romantic or sexual partners to fulfill your needs, often disregarding the impact on your current relationship. This betrayal is a significant breach of trust and causes deep emotional pain for your partner.

- *Lies and Deceptions:* You might tend to keep secrets and lie about your actions or intentions, which further eats away trust. This constant deception leaves your partner feeling continually betrayed and unsure of what to believe.

Note: Note everyone with narcissistic tendencies will be unfaithful to their partner but the traits associated with this trait naturally nurture cheating.

---

[6] https://psychcentral.com/disorders/narcissism-and-sexual-addiction

Long-Term Psychological Effects

Also, your behavior can have extreme long-term psychological effects on your partner. Understanding these effects is important to help you make positive changes in your relationship. They include:

- *Anxiety and Depression*: The constant stress and emotional turmoil you create in your relationship can lead your partner to develop anxiety, depression, and other mental health issues.

- *Low Self-Esteem:* Your continuous criticism and devaluation can significantly erode your partner's self-esteem, making them feel unworthy and unloved.

- *Trauma and PTSD*: In severe cases, the emotional abuse you inflict can result in trauma or post-traumatic stress disorder (PTSD) for your partner, requiring professional therapy for recovery.

These effects are likely to be similar in all your personal relationships.

Other than your personal relationships, your professional ones will also likely suffer due to narcissism. Let's find out how:

Effects of Narcissist Tendencies on Your Professional Relationships

Some of the ways in which having NPD can affect your career include:

Lack of Team Collaboration

Whether employed or an entrepreneur, teamwork is essential for growth and prosperity. However, your need to be the center of attention and receive admiration can significantly hinder effective teamwork. Since you feed on attention, you might dominate most discussions, which can prevent others from sharing their ideas and contributing to their and the team's success.

Additionally, you may dismiss colleagues' or employees' ideas outright, undervaluing their input and making them feel unappreciated. Also, you might tend to take credit for your colleagues' or employees' work, which leaves them and the team resenting you.

These actions tend to lead to a toxic work environment where your team members lose motivation and become unwilling to cooperate. Without collaboration, your department, organization, or business loses creativity and innovation, eventually affecting your growth.

Conflict and Tension

To improve workplace dynamics, learning to accept feedback gracefully and take responsibility for your actions is essential. When you accept your mistakes and use them to grow, you reduce the chances of having avoidable conflicts and build stronger, more respectful working relationships. This, in turn, leads to a more positive and collaborative working environment, which benefits both your professional growth and the team's success.

However, this is almost impossible because your hypersensitivity to criticism and tendency to blame others can create significant conflict and tension in the workplace. Colleagues, partners, or employees may find it challenging to provide you with constructive feedback, fearing negative reactions or retaliation. This can lead to many unresolved issues, damaging your team's cohesion.

Additionally, constantly shifting blame to your team can eat away trust and respect among team members, making collaboration difficult. Colleagues and team might become reluctant to work closely with you, leading to isolation and further misunderstandings. This behavior hinders your professional growth and affects the company or business's overall productivity and morale.

Poor Leadership Qualities

If you hold a leadership position[7], your narcissistic traits might result in an authoritarian and unsupportive management style. This can demotivate your team, reduce morale, and increase turnover rates. When employees feel undervalued and controlled, they are less likely to be productive and more likely to seek opportunities elsewhere.

An authoritarian leadership style can suppress creativity and discourage team members from sharing their ideas, leading to a lack of innovation and growth. Your team might feel they are working in a hostile environment where their contributions are neither recognized nor appreciated. This can lead to disengagement and a decline in overall team performance.

Good leaders inspire and support their teams by ensuring a positive and inclusive environment. When you practice an empathetic and inclusive leadership style, you improve your team's performance and satisfaction. Other effective tools for providing support and boosting morale and productivity as a leader, leading to unity and growth, include open communication and recognizing achievements.

---

[7] https://www.ncbi.nlm.nih.gov/pmc/articles/PMC9301298/

Career Stagnation

While you may initially succeed due to your confidence and assertiveness, your narcissistic traits can ultimately <u>hinder your long-term career growth</u>[8]. Initially, these qualities might help you stand out and achieve quick wins. However, over time, the negative impact of your behavior can become more apparent to colleagues and superiors.

Your tendency to dominate conversations, dismiss others' ideas, and take credit for team achievements can create a toxic work environment. This behavior can strain your professional relationships and lead to a lack of trust, making colleagues and superiors reluctant to collaborate with you or consider you for promotions. As a result, you may find yourself stuck in your current position and unable to advance.

Here are some questions to help you reflect and recognize the damage narcissism has done or might do to you, helping you understand the need for you to stay true to and determined in this journey.

---

[8]

<u>https://www.researchgate.net/publication/271224682_Narcissism_and_career_success_Occupational_self-efficacy_and_career_engagement_as_mediators</u>

Question 1: Do you often feel the need for constant admiration and validation from your partner?

Answer Choices:

A. Yes, frequently

B. Occasionally

C. Rarely

(Reflection: If you answered A or B, think of how this might overshadow your partner's needs, leading to emotional neglect.)

Question 2: Have you ever used tactics like gaslighting or emotional blackmail to control your partner?

Answer Choices:

A. Yes

B. Sometimes

C. No

(Reflection: For example, suppose you cheated on your partner and they confronted you. In this case, reflect on how you didn't care to listen to their feelings by saying something like, "I was going through a lot you wouldn't understand.")

Question 3: Do you find your behavior swinging between idealizing and devaluing your partner?

Answer Choices:

A. Yes, often

B. Occasionally

C. Never

(**Reflection:** If you answered A or B, consider the anxiety and insecurity this creates for your partner.)

Question 4: Do you become defensive and shift blame during conflicts?

Answer Choices:

A. Yes, frequently

B. Sometimes

C. No

(**Reflection:** In our case of unfaithfulness, you could have shifted the blame by saying something like, "You are always busy with work and the kids to a point you don't put us first anymore, and you do have a part to play in my actions." Recognizing defensiveness can help you work towards healthier conflict resolution.)

Question 5: Have you isolated your partner from their friends and family?

Answer Choices:

A. Yes

B. Sometimes

C. No

(*Reflection*: Reflect on how increasing your partner's dependency can harm their well-being and your relationship, keeping in mind that they have other non-romantic relationships that they must nurture.)

Question 6: Do you notice signs of anxiety or depression in your partner, possibly due to your behavior?

Answer Choices:

A. Yes

B. Not Sure

C. No

(*Reflection*: Recognizing the impact of your actions on your partner's mental health is a crucial step towards positive change.)

Question 7: Are you hypersensitive to criticism and tend to shift blame in the workplace?

Answer Choices:

A. Yes

B. Sometimes

C. No

3. Poor Leadership Qualities

Question 8: Do you adopt an authoritarian leadership style, controlling everything your team does?

Answer Choices:

A. Yes

B. Occasionally

C. No

(Reflection: If you answered A or B, consider how this can demotivate your team and increase turnover rates.)

Question 9: Have you noticed that your career has stagnated despite a good start?

Answer Choices:

A. Yes

B. Sometimes

C. No

(**Reflection**: Consider how your narcissistic traits might be hindering your long-term professional growth. Can you say that your narcissistic traits have been standing between you and career or entrepreneurial prosperity?)

As you can see, not working to improve and eliminate these unhealthy traits does more harm than good. But worry not because, in the following chapters, we will comprehensively cover the most effective strategies to help change your life and those around you.

Before then, let's find out what might be the triggers to your narcissist traits and how to deal with them in the next part.

Part III

Self-Awareness and Managing Triggers

Part III marks the beginning of your journey to overcoming narcissism. This guide takes a unique and effective approach that aims to deal with the issue from its root cause.

So, how do you do that?

Recognizing your own narcissistic triggers is the first step towards managing them effectively, so here, we will explore tools and strategies for identifying and understanding these triggers. After that, you will learn how to manage these triggers to help reduce the impact of narcissistic behavior on your life and relationships.

When you are able to notice your triggers and manage them, you will have an easier time understanding and implementing the strategies provided to unlearn your narcissist behaviors, replacing them with healthier ones.

Let's get started!

Chapter 4: Recognize Your Triggers

To stop being a narcissist or engaging in narcissistic behaviors, the first thing you ought to do should be to become aware of your triggers.

How To Recognize Your Narcissistic Triggers

First, whenever you engage in narcissistic behavior, whether that behavior is narcissistic rage, demeaning a loved one, manipulative crying, silent treatment, etc., you do so because something has triggered you.

Elinor Greenberg, Ph.D., CGP, is a world-renowned Gestalt therapy professional who teaches other psychotherapists how to diagnose and treat personality disorders such as NDP, borderline personality disorder, and Schizoid Personality Disorder.

She notes that triggers for narcissistic behaviors are any words, behaviors, or situations that cause strong negative feelings within you, such that to rebalance your sense of self-esteem, you act out.

For instance, you are likely to act out when your partner does something you consider displeasing. This 'something' could perhaps be mentioning how a particular way of dressing does not compliment you and instead makes you look clownish. In such a situation, you may lash out because the statement has hurt your fragile ego and self-esteem.

Because triggers are the situations or circumstances that cause you to engage in narcissistic tendencies, to get started on the path to freedom from narcissism, you need to become intimately aware of them.

To do this, the first thing you need to do is whip out your notebook, and on it, write down all the situations, circumstances, words, and behaviors that cause you to engage in narcissistic behaviors towards the people in your life —only to regret it later.

At this point, do not worry about the details; just engage in free-form writing detailing the things that stir negative feelings within you and cause you to act out intensely against someone you believe has said something hurtful to your self-esteem.

Your list of triggers could look like:

- When someone of 'low status' asks challenging questions, especially ones whose answers you don't know.

- When someone of 'low status,' such as a 'waiter' or repairman, fails to treat you with reverence or serve you as 'fast as someone of your high caliber deserves.'

- When your partner ignores you

- When someone criticizes your opinion instead of treating it with the importance it deserves

The more attention you pay to yourself, the more aware you shall become, which is a good thing because awareness —of your triggers and your reactions to them— is the first step to overcoming narcissistic tendencies.

Besides free-form writing your triggers in your self-development notebook, you can use the strategies below to become more aware of the things that trigger your narcissistic behaviors or tendencies.

Become Aware of Emotional Triggers

Here is the truth —you can take it, right?

Most of the things that cause you to behave narcissistically are internal more than they are external. We call these emotional triggers.

You behave narcissistically towards something (and someone) you consider offensive not because the occurrence is always offensive but because you DEEM IT or THINK it is offensive.

In essence, this means you act out narcissistically when an occurrence or something someone says does not sit well with you or align with the mental models you have created. What a person or situation stirs within you —emotional triggers— are why you act reactively: because something (or someone) has hurt your emotions and bruised your self-image (and fragile ego, sorry to say).

By becoming more aware of your emotional triggers, how certain things and situations make you feel, and how you react once you feel these things, you can manage your reactions better. After all, you cannot manage something of which you are unaware.

When thinking about which emotions trigger your narcissistic behaviors, keep in mind that what counts are all the things, circumstances, words, or actions that stir up negative feelings within you and cause you to want to lash out. Common examples of emotional triggers known to cause narcissistic behavior include:

* Someone rejecting you.

* Someone leaving you (or the threat that they will).

* Helplessness over painful situations.

* Someone discounting or ignoring you.

* Someone being unavailable to you.

* Someone giving you a disapproving look.

* Someone blaming or shaming you.

* Someone being judgmental or critical of you.

* Someone being too busy to make time for you.

* Someone not appearing to be happy to see you.

Courtesy of Margaret Paul, Ph.D.

Before you can stop being a narcissist —or acting narcissistically— and give up the need to control everything, including your relationships, you need to become intimately aware of your emotional triggers. The reason for this is simple: while you can blame your reactions on external circumstances, the truth is that you act or react the way you do because of what you feel —your emotions.

Observe What Your Body Is Feeling

If you are attentive enough, you will notice that whenever you are about to act narcissistically, your body reacts to your emotions in a specific way. For instance, when someone fails to treat you like a 'demi-god,' your body is likely to tense, your breathing quickens, and, depending on the offensiveness you attach to the 'insult,' your body temperature may rise too.

By paying attention to your body, you can become more aware of the various bodily changes that occur before you engage in narcissistic behavior.

Pay Attention To Your Thoughts and Monologue

Again, all narcissistic behaviors are a result of feeling offended. You take offense not because something someone says or does is offensive but because your inner monologue tells you that you should take offense. Remember that thoughts lead to emotions; emotions, on the other hand, lead to reactions.

By paying attention to your thoughts and inner monologue, you can become more aware of instances where what you are thinking influences your behavior and causes you to act controlling and manipulative towards loved ones and other people. Aim to become more aware of which thoughts cause you to act (or react) in ways others would consider self-centered or self-absorbed.

Taking note of the internal and external actions, words, and behaviors that cause you to act or react narcissistically towards the people in your life is the first step to managing narcissism and then gradually overcoming it.

The more aware you become of your triggers, the more capable you will be in managing them. Moreover, by becoming aware of the things that cause you to act self-centered toward loved ones, you can give yourself a momentary chance to choose another, more empathic reaction —instead of a narcissistic one.

Practice Meditation

As you will learn later, to beat narcissism and stop being controlling in relationships, one of the things you need to do once you become aware of your triggers is to create space between the trigger and your reactions.

You can choose a more empathetic reaction by creating this momentary pause. Unfortunately, becoming aware enough to create a space between triggers and your reaction is not easy, but it becomes easier with time. One way you can get here is through meditation.

Meditation is many things.

With narcissism, however, meditation is a strategic tool you can use to cultivate moment-to-moment awareness, gain a more profound understanding of yourself, and detach from experiences by observing them nonjudgmentally.

As you practice meditation consistently and master remaining attentive in situations without changing or reacting to them, you will be able to manage challenging emotions and deliberate with your actions and reactions.

Additionally, because meditation helps improve your self-awareness, by practicing it consistently, you shall learn more about the emotional wounds that led to the formation of the narcissistic self as well as the factors that trigger narcissistic behaviors.

Practicing meditation will help you learn how to detach from experiences that trigger your narcissistic reactions. It will help you observe them nonjudgmentally as passing conditions, which will help you realize that you don't have to react to every narcissistic impulse you experience.

When you develop the ability to observe impulses such as narcissistic rage, painful emotions, self-centeredness, arrogance, super-minded thinking, etc., without being judgmental or reactive, the pause created between impulse and reaction gives you control over choosing your reaction.

This pause, and the control it brings about, can prove very useful against habitual narcissistic tendencies because once there is that pause, you can choose a more empathic reaction.

The great thing about all this is that in addition to helping you relate to, instead of reacting to, your thoughts, meditation helps you become aware of the narcissistic stories you tell yourself.

Becoming aware of these stories allows you to become more intimate with the mental models that you have created. In cases where these models don't serve you as well as you would like them to, awareness makes it easier to change them by choosing another model whenever the trigger for one model manifests.

Fortunately, practicing meditation so that you can notice your narcissistic mental models and where they manifest and choose a better response is not too challenging.

NOTE: Meditation alone cannot help you stop being a narcissist. What it does is help you become more self-aware of yourself, your actions, reactions, and how they affect others.

Because of the moment-to-moment self-awareness it creates, it helps you notice triggers and instances where you are likely to act controlling —or about to engage in other narcissistic behaviors. From this awareness, since you are committed to being a better person, you can choose a more positive action/reaction to a stimulus.

You can use a guided meditation app such as Headspace or Calm or practice the following meditation practice for five minutes three times a day to cultivate a more profound sense of inner and external awareness.

1. Get into a comfortable sitting position; you can lie down, too, but sitting is better. Sit up straight, but make sure you are not too rigid; maintain the back's natural curvature.

2. Close your eyes —you can also gaze downwards— and draw in a few deep, calming breaths. These first few deep breaths aim to get a feel for and relax the body physically, mentally, and emotionally. Pay attention to areas where you can feel any tightness or tension and breathe into them. Notice the state of your mind, whether calm or turbulent, and your emotional state.

3. Focus on the breath. Notice as much as you can about the in-breath and the sensations experienced as you do. Remember that when meditating to gain awareness, the aim is not to change anything but to observe! Observe your breath without changing a thing or reacting in any

way: simply let your awareness rest on the breath. Do the same thing with the out-breath! Rest your awareness on it and notice all you can about it.

4. When the mind wanders off in thought, which it will do, notice where it wandered off to, momentarily rest your awareness on where the mind went, and then refocus on observing the breath once again. The more attuned to your breath, the more self-aware you become.

5. After observing your breath for a while, expand your awareness. First, focus on sounds within your meditation space and then on your thoughts. Observe them without any judgment.

6. Since the aim of this meditation is to gain insight into your narcissistic tendencies, call to mind any traumas you think are the primary causes of your narcissism and observe them without judgment. Let them play out in your mind as if they are stories observed by a third party.

7. Likewise, call to mind instances where you know you are prone to acting narcissistically, controlling, or manipulative, and think of the triggers that cause these behaviors. Again, remember to observe this nonjudgmentally, without wanting to change a thing.

8. Call to mind how you would like to act instead (of narcissistically) and focus on priming your mind for the behavioral change by repeating a mantra. For instance, let us assume that whenever your partner does not ask about your day, you get angry and act out angrily. In this instance, to use meditation to prime your mind for behavioral change, call to mind how you routinely react to this situation.

9. However, because you are committed to behavioral change this time, think about the positive thing you want to do instead and turn it into a mantra. For example, if you want to take a few calming breaths and then shift the focus on your partner, you can say, "whenever my partner does not ask me about my day, I will take ten deep breathes. Once I feel calmer, I will ask her about her day and listen attentively."

10. By priming your mind in this manner, you will create a neural association that will help you become aware of the trigger that causes you to engage in narcissistic tendencies. By creating this neural association, you will remember to engage in the alternative behavior instead of the narcissistic one whenever the trigger occurs.

As mentioned, meditation is not a cure-all solution to narcissism. Additionally, for it to work and help you become a better person, someone more compassionate and empathic, you need to be committed to self-betterment.

Action Steps:

Using what you have learned from this section about triggers, pay attention to yourself more closely and notice which internal and external factors cause you to behave narcissistically towards the people in your life.

Here is a practical worksheet to help you do that:

Action 1: Identify Your Triggers:

Exercise: List several, say 5, recent situations or experiences where you felt the urge to act out narcissistically (refer to the narcissistic behaviors we discussed in chapter 1). Describe what happened, who was involved, and how you felt.

Example: "Last week, my mum criticized my cooking in front of our friends. I felt embarrassed and angry."

_____

_____

_____

_____

Action 2: Practice Emotional Awareness:

Exercise: What emotions do you frequently experience just before you engage in narcissistic behavior? List at least three emotions and explain how they make you feel.

Example: "I often feel anger, inadequacy, and jealousy. Anger makes me want to lash out, inadequacy makes me feel unworthy, and jealousy makes me feel less than others."

_____

_____

_____

_____

Action 3: Note the Bodily Sensations You Experience when Triggered in Different Situations:

Exercise: At any calm moment during the day, think back to a recent situation that triggered you. Close your eyes and recall how your body felt. Note down any physical sensations (e.g., flushed face, clenched fists, tightened chest, sweating, increased heartrate).

Example: "When my coworker ignored my idea, I felt a knot in my stomach, and my hands started shaking."

_____

_____

_____

Action 4: Thought Patterns:

Exercise: Reflect on your self-talk during a triggering event. What are the recurring thoughts or beliefs that come up? Write down these thoughts.

Example: "I often think, *'They don't respect me'* or *'I am not good enough.'"*

_____

_____

_____

Action 5: Free-Form Writing:

Exercise: Spend about 10 minutes writing about what triggers you. Do not censor yourself. Focus on any situations, words, or behaviors that provoke a strong reaction in you.

Prompt: "Write about when someone's behavior made you feel insignificant. How did you react, and what thoughts and feelings were you having?"

_____

_____

_____

_____

_____

_____

_____

_____

_____

_____

_____

Action 6: Observe Your Reactions:

Exercise: Describe how you typically respond to different triggers. Do you manipulate, lash out, or withdraw?

Example: "When my partner doesn't compliment me, I give them the silent treatment to make them feel guilty."

_____

_____

_____

Once you recognize and acknowledge your triggers, you will be better able to manage them and overcome narcissism.

Chapter 5: Learn How To Manage Your Triggers

Having learned about your triggers in Chapter 4, *the things that cause you to act controlling and narcissistically towards your loved ones and other people*, the first step to starting your journey to self-betterment and becoming better placed is to manage these triggers.

NOTE: Whenever we use the term 'act narcissistically,' we mean whenever you engage in narcissistic behavior such as narcissistic rage, demeaning and putting others down, not showing empathy in situations that call for it, acting cocky and manipulative, etc.

To manage your triggers and, in so doing, become capable of inserting a momentary pause between a stimulus and narcissistic behavior or tendencies, use the following strategies:

Relate

Relating the things that cause you to act narcissistically to your childhood and mental models is a crucial step to overcoming narcissism.

As discussed in the chapter on the known causes of narcissism, narcissism is usually a result of childhood experiences that may have caused you to create faulty mental models, thought processes, and an inflated self-image/ego. Because of this, you must relate your triggers to chief childhood experiences you think (or believe) are what led to the formation of a narcissistic personality.

Here, it's vital that as you relate your triggers with childhood experiences, you practice being openly honest with yourself; you must take off the blinders of the ego and go deep.

Take each trigger on your list and question it. Ask yourself prodding questions that help you learn things such as the first instance when you noticed the trigger, what caused you to adopt that reaction, what about the trigger stands out and causes you to react manipulatively, etc.

The more awareness you have of the factors behind why some things cause you to become defensive, act cocky, embellish your achievements, etc., the easier it shall be to get to their root cause. Additionally, it will be easier to relate them to the childhood experiences that may have caused you to 'feel better than,' more entitled, or 'more special.'

Dig as deep as possible, and as you do, be patient and kind to yourself. Also, keep in mind that introspecting to relate your triggers and narcissistic tendencies with your childhood experiences may bring about some internal resistance and emotional pain. As such, the process may take time.

A journal will come in handy here. In addition to being a tool to monitor your triggers, it (a journal) will also help you work back to the root causes of these triggers, your emotions, etc. Moreover, you can use it as a safe place to vent, which, although it may seem non-essential, will help ensure that you rarely —if ever— act out in narcissistic rage.

As you journal, engage in consciousness journaling by writing about your experiences without editing anything. Your journal is a safe place where you can let go and be a 'diva' if being a diva makes you feel good about yourself. Write uninhibitedly; something you write could prove the secret to making positive changes in your life.

Accept

As a self-aware narcissist who knows that being so could be ruining your relationships and harming your well-being, you are likely to notice the formation of negative self-sentiments.

When you notice the formation of negative self-sentiments, accept your triggers and feelings, and do not try to hide them —or from them. Remember that you have narcissistic tendencies because something happened that caused you to develop a false protective persona that protects the fragile, real you.

Instead, accept your triggers and the resultant narcissistic behavior they cause by reminding yourself that you are a human being. Therefore, there is no reason to strive towards perfection when we know for a fact that human perfection is a fallacy.

Remind yourself that having triggers that irk and cause you to act out is part of what it means to be a human being. Remind yourself that having triggers that cause you to act narcissistically does not mean you are a wicked person. Like most people, it means that you need to work towards self-betterment and be more empathetic towards others.

Practicing this level of self-acceptance will allow you to realize that the triggers you consider triggers are one-time occurrences that you have reacted to consistently, so much so that they have become habitual. In the same way, these triggers cause you to act a certain way, and if you are committed to it, you can teach yourself how to react to them positively.

For instance, if failing to receive a constant stream of compliments from your partner leaves you feeling 'unworshipped,' accept that this trigger causes you to feel and perhaps react a certain way. Doing this will help you realize that you are human, which is why you are feeling the way you do.

Out of this awareness and understanding, you will realize that you control your actions and behaviors. This realization will empower you so that instead of beating yourself up for being narcissistic, you can think about what you can do differently.

Consider The Consequences

As mentioned several times, one of the hallmark characteristics of narcissistic personality disorder is that as a narcissist, your actions and behaviors are always out of self-absorption: you never consider how other people may feel about or react to the things you do or say.

This lack, or low levels of empathy, is why you never hesitate to manipulate or use other people to get your way. It is also why, when a chance to show others how superior, better, or exceptional you are, you never let a chance to rail on someone pass you by, even when doing so would amount to adding salt to a festering wound.

As you work to manage the internal and external triggers that cause you to act narcissistically, especially towards loved ones and people who care about you, get into the habit of reminding yourself that, like you, other people have feelings. What you say or do hurts them!

Unfortunately, the fact that you are a narcissist means because you are your primary concern, you are prone to acting without thinking about how your actions, words, or behaviors affect others. To stop being narcissistic and self-centered, you need to commit yourself to the interruption of this habit. Instead, you need to emphasize thinking about your responses and their consequences so that where they are narcissistic, you can adopt another, more empathic response.

When you practice moment-to-moment self-awareness, it becomes easier to recognize instances where you are prone to responding narcissistically —and the things that trigger you. Out of this awareness and your commitment to becoming a better, less narcissistic person, you shall have pauses that you can use to determine how acting a certain way will affect your loved ones and the people in your life.

The more you use these pauses or moments to consider the consequences of your narcissistic behavior, the more control you will have over it, and the more capable you shall be of instigating positive behavioral changes.

An example we can use to illustrate this is when your partner talks about their enjoyable or tiresome day, it triggers your desire to change the conversation to your day. In this example, you can create a momentary pause by becoming aware of this trigger and how changing the point of conversation shall affect your partner. This momentary pause can allow you to act empathetically instead of reacting narcissistically.

Elinor Greenberg says that when you practice awareness of the causes of your narcissistic behaviors and practice delaying impulsive reactions by thinking about the consequences of your responses, you can interrupt the unwanted, narcissistic behavior in favor of a better, more empathetic one.

When you take that momentary pause to think about how your actions, reactions, and behaviors affect others, you will realize that your narcissistic tendencies are hurting the people who care for you. Thinking about this will encourage you to be more loving and empathetic towards them by changing your reactions to positive ones.

Additionally, thinking about the consequences of your narcissistic habits will help you stop thinking about yourself all the time, which will herald you into the next step of self-growth: being more empathetic by practicing emotional intelligence.

Worksheet

Action 1: Relate:

Exercise: Reflect on one of the recent circumstances where you showed narcissistic traits or refer to any you wrote in the previous chapter. Write about the trigger and relate it to a childhood experience.

Question: When was the first time you remember feeling this way? For example, if criticism makes you defensive or being told no causes you to lash out, recall how you reacted to criticism or not as a child.

_____

_____

_____

_____

_____

_____

_____

_____

Action 2: Accept:

Exercise: Practice self-acceptance by acknowledging a narcissistic behavior you caught yourself exhibiting this week.

Question: How did you feel about yourself when you noticed this behavior?

Example: If you felt upset for not receiving praise from your friends for your new haircut, write down why it affected you and remind yourself it's okay to have these feelings.

_____

_____

_____

_____

_____

_____

_____

_____

Action 3: Think of the Consequences:

Exercise: From now on, during conversations, take your time before you react. Pause and consider the impact of your reaction or response on the other person.

Question: How would your response affect their feelings? For example, if you feel the need to shift your attention to yourself when your friend is sharing their experience at work, take a moment before that and think about how it would make them feel.

_____

_____

_____

_____

_____

_____

_____

_____

Action 4: Journaling Prompts:

Reflect: Write about a trigger you managed well recently and the steps you took.

_____

_____

_____

_____

_____

_____

_____

_____

Plan: Identify a common trigger and outline how you will handle it differently next time.

_____

_____

_____

_____

_____

_____

_____

_____

Use this worksheet to manage each of your triggers, making one positive change at a time.

Part IV

Emotional Growth and Empathy

In this part, we will focus on two critical aspects of emotional well-being: empathy and controlling your narcissistic rage.

Empathy is a powerful tool that can make a big difference in how we relate to others and how they perceive us. It involves being able to understand and share the feelings of others, and the best way to do this is by improving our emotional intelligence. When we become more aware of our own emotions and those of others, we can communicate better and build healthier relationships that are not controlled by narcissistic traits.

And since narcissist rage is one of the most destructive emotional responses that can prevent you from practicing empathy, we will also discuss strategies for managing and controlling it.

By improving your emotional intelligence and learning to control your narcissist rage, you will notice that you portray fewer narcissistic traits and even be able to relate with those around you better.

Chapter 6: Becoming More Empathetic and Controlling Your Narcissistic Rage

Embracing Empathy by Improving Your Emotional Intelligence

Because of its focus on the exaltation of the self, narcissism hinders your ability to practice emotional intelligence, which is the ability to comprehend, manage, and positively use emotions, like effective communication, dealing well with stressful situations, and empathizing with others.

Narcissism, as discussed in an earlier chapter, usually develops when you create destructive coping mechanisms to conditions, actions, or words that you do not align with your self-perception.

Developing your emotional intelligence helps counteract this and rewrite this mental narrative by making you more empathetic or capable of putting yourself in someone else's shoes, which makes it easier to act in a manner that helps defuse relationship conflict.

It helps you build a better connection with your emotions and feelings so that you can use them to make better, more informed decisions. Additionally, a well-developed emotional quotient can help you develop better relationships because it helps you become comfortable with your emotions. It also builds social intelligence, which can help you better deal with people positively.

To build emotional intelligence so that you can become more empathetic and therefore capable of considering others, apply the following strategies:

Practice Self-Management

As a recovering narcissist, practicing emotional self-management could prove the secret to beating it for good.

Emotional self-management involves using awareness of your emotions and feelings to decide which behaviors to engage in based on how constructive they are. For instance, when a trigger causes your narcissistic rage to flare up, a well-developed ability to self-manage is what allows you to think clearly about the emotion and the effects of acting upon the impulse.

Emotional self-management allows you to be in stressful, challenging situations without necessarily overreacting to them, allowing you to practice self-control.

Strategies that can help you practice emotional self-management so that you don't engage in narcissistic, controlling behavior toward your loved ones include:

- **Pausing:** As discussed earlier, when you pause to think about the effects of your reactions, actions, and behaviors on the people that matter to you, it gives you a chance to consider. For a narcissist, consideration is critical, which is why pausing is integral to self-management.

- **Deep breath:** To manage challenging emotions and situations that often cause you to engage in controlling, manipulative behavior towards your partner or loved ones, you can use deep breathing (or the meditation practice we discussed earlier). Deep breathing gives you moment-to-moment awareness, which makes it easier to observe challenging emotions as they arise and to let them fall and fade without reacting to them in any way. It also eases tension.

Another self-management strategy you can use is shifting your attentional focus away from the trigger and your characteristic narcissistic reaction to the new, more empathetic way you would like to act.

Become More Self-Aware

Emotions are an inescapable part of life, as are challenges and disappointments. Self-awareness is essential for freedom from narcissism because it allows you to practice emotional self-management and become more empathetic. It also gives you a connection that allows you to see how your emotions and feelings lead to narcissistic behavior and actions.

Becoming more self-aware allows you to become conscious of how the rise of one emotion triggers the rise of another and how strong your emotions are at any given moment. This awareness is essential to practicing emotional intelligence because it allows you to become attentive enough to notice when your feelings and emotions lead to impulsive behaviors such as narcissistic manipulation and anger.

Meditation is one of the best ways to become more self-aware, and we've already discussed it at length. Other strategies you can use to become more self-aware include:

- **Practicing objectivity:** As a recovering narcissist, you will struggle with looking at yourself objectively, especially once you take off the blinders of the narcissistic self. No matter how challenging it is, you must put in the effort.

  The more objectively you see yourself, the easier it shall be to recognize and heal the wounds that led to the formation of your narcissistic self so that you can learn to accept and love the real you. Some tips you can use to practice self-objectivity include journaling and being honest with yourself.

- **Practice daily self-reflection:** Set aside 10-60 minutes of your day to engage in self-reflection. Use this time as you wish, but make sure you use a portion of it engaged in critical self-reflection related to how you acted in circumstances where you would have otherwise acted controlling and narcissistically.

Practice Social Awareness

Social awareness is the ability to identify and interpret nonverbal communication. When you become socially aware, you become capable of noticing how others feel, or, in this case, notice how others react to what you say and do.

While social awareness may not seem like such a big deal, it is because when you notice how the people around you react to your interactions, you can become aware of how your behaviors affect others. For instance, by becoming more socially aware, you can notice when others show nonverbal cues that indicate that you have engaged in a hurtful behavior that others would consider narcissistic, controlling, or manipulative.

You can practice and improve your social awareness skills by practicing mindfulness meditation. When you practice mindfulness and become more self-aware, you can use that awareness to observe situations nonjudgmentally. Doing this will allow you to detach from the egotistical, narcissistic self and see things, including your actions and reactions, as they are.

Other useful strategies you can use to improve your social awareness include:

- **Active listening:** To reduce your tendency to control, manipulate, and drive conversations back to you, practice active listening by paying attention to other people and using the support-response to ask questions that probe others to talk more about themselves. Yes, this will breed some internal friction and take time to get used to, but the more you do it, the less self-absorbed you shall gradually become.

- **Paraphrase:** Paraphrasing is a communication strategy that works excellently well and helps you develop empathic listening. It involves using self-created words to parrot what someone has said as a way to show that you are listening and understanding what someone is saying or has said. For instance, if your partner says, "Today was so tiresome," you could say, "What made today so tiresome for you?" As you can see, this response paraphrases the initial comment, and because it's a support-response, using it —and others like it— will gradually help you become less self-centered.

By improving your level of emotional intelligence, you will learn to put yourself in other people's shoes. You will be able to be more empathetic where you would have otherwise acted narcissistically and show genuine interest in others.

While this process will not be easy and require a willingness to do things you have never imagined your narcissistic self would allow you to, the effort shall be worth it in the end.

Learning How to Control Narcissistic Rage

Narcissistic rage is a prevalent narcissistic behavior. It usually manifests in two ways: silence or silent treatment used as a tool for manipulation and intense outbursts of anger. In both instances, narcissistic rage happens when a trigger, perhaps a person, situation, or action, harms or threatens your fragile sense of self-esteem and ego.

As you gradually work towards self-betterment and overwriting your narcissistic tendencies with empathetic responses, you need to learn how to control narcissistic rage, especially when you fail to get the admiration and attention you crave.

To overcome narcissistic rage, you need to adopt a gradual approach. If you use the awareness and empathy techniques we have discussed thus far, you should be able to do this —it will still require effort.

Adding on to everything we have discussed, employ the following strategies that explicitly seek to help you deal with narcissistic rage:

Delay Response

Narcissistic rage is usually a conditioned reaction to stimuli. To stop engaging in it and the controlling, manipulative behaviors that drive it, the first thing you need to do is cultivate mindful awareness so that you can become aware of moments when your narcissistic rage flares up.

By being aware, you shall be able to delay response, perhaps not on the first try, but the more you practice it, the more aware you shall become of the triggers that cause you to act out angrily or engage in silent treatment.

Practicing delayed response will take time to get used to, but when you create the mental association to do it, the easier it will be with time.

Calm Down

In the fits of narcissistic rage, thinking with clarity becomes challenging, and you are likely to do or say something regretful. To avoid that, whenever you notice narcissistic rage building up, take a few deep, calming breaths. Being aware enough to engage in deep breathing will interrupt your habitual response and calm down your nervous system so that you can 'think straight.' Combined with meditation, deep breathing can be a highly effective way to stop reacting with narcissistic rage.

Rationalize

Narcissistic rage is an emotional reaction to feeling hurt or let down. As alluded to in an earlier chapter of this book, emotions are not good or bad; they just are. What matters is whether and how you react to them.

To ensure that feeling hurt does not turn into a full-blown episode of narcissistic rage, practice rationalizing. The best way to rationalize is to ask yourself probing questions related to the outcome of your actions/reactions.

Seek Understanding

Sometimes, you might misunderstand situations or circumstances, and this can trigger narcissistic responses. Therefore, anytime you feel the onset of rage, take a moment and try to understand everything from the other person's point of view. Other than helping cultivate empathy, pausing to understand the situation or issue from other people's perspectives will help reduce your anger and give you time to find a thoughtful, measured, and helpful response.

But how exactly do you understand others' points of view?

This entails you recognizing that people are not always out to belittle or harm you. Their words and actions are a result of their feelings, circumstances, beliefs, motivations, or thoughts concerning the situation, and it is only fair to consider them to find a balance and solution that favors everyone involved. This can help you realize that the trigger may not be as threatening or personal as you initially thought.

When you practice empathy to understand others, you avoid conflicts and promote open and constructive communication, leading to mutual respect and healthy interactions.

Practice Self-Compassion

Often, narcissistic rage comes from deep-seated feelings of fear and inadequacy, and practicing self-compassion can help address these issues. Self-compassion simply means treating yourself with kindness when you feel intense emotions, fail, or face a challenge. Do you see the advice you would give a friend or loved one in a situation that makes them feel inadequate? Well, take that advice, too.

It is okay to feel hurt, and the feelings associated with narcissistic traits don't define your worth. The best thing to do is be gentle with yourself. Whenever you catch yourself using these unhealthy traits, recognize your feelings without judgment. Doing this can prevent you from raging impulsively, allowing you to respond more calmly and constructively.

Note: We will discuss this in detail later.

Engage in Physical Activity

Sometimes, you only need a short run, a good swim, or a yoga session to help you feel better and boost your mood. Narcissist rage is usually accompanied by intense energy, and physical activities help provide a constructive outlet for your built-up tension and stress. Actually, it has been proven that regular exercise stimulates the production of the hormone endorphins[9], which reduces depression and feelings of anger and frustration and improves overall mood.

Incorporating physical activity into your routine helps you create a healthy habit that supports emotional regulation. Whether it's the meditative nature of yoga or evening jog, these activities help calm your mind and body.

Also, they serve as a moment of mindfulness, allowing you to focus on your breathing and your body. This, in turn, allows you to distance yourself from triggers and reactive thoughts,

---

[9] https://www.webmd.com/depression/exercise-depression

helping manage immediate outbursts and building long-term resilience against stress.

In other words, making physical activity part of your life leads to a more controlled and balanced emotional state, which enables you to approach triggering or challenging situations with greater calm and clarity.

Worksheet:

Action 1: Reflection Exercise:

Exercise: Take 10 minutes each day to write about your emotional responses in different challenging situations. Do you often feel frustrated or angry? And how do these feelings make you act narcissistically? Ask yourself, *"What triggered these emotions? How did I react, and why? What could I have done differently?"*

_____

_____

_____

_____

_____

_____

_____

_____

_____

_____

_____

_____

_____

Action 2: Practice Empathy:

Exercise: Choose one situation or conversation daily to practice active listening without cutting in with your opinions or experiences. Only focus on understanding the other person's feelings and perspective. Afterward, write down three key points you learned about their feelings or situation that you hadn't considered before:

_____

_____

_____

_____

_____

_____

_____

_____

_____

_____

_____

_____

_____

Action 3: Create Mindfulness Moments During Your Day:

Exercise: Anytime you notice yourself becoming defensive or feel tension rising, pause and take three slow, deep breaths. Notice (and note down) how this practice helps you feel and react to the situation:

_____

_____

_____

_____

_____

_____

_____

_____

_____

_____

_____

Action 4: Self-Compassion Exercise:

Exercise: Come up with affirmations or mantras that resonate with you and breathe kindness into your life. It could be as simple as *"I am learning and growing," "It's okay to make mistakes," "I am smart,"* or *"I am worthy of true love."* Repeat it/them to yourself whenever you feel your narcissistic triggers poking your emotions. Also, write down your chosen mantra and place it somewhere you will see it often.

_____

_____

_____

_____

_____

_____

_____

_____

_____

_____

_____

_____

Action 5: Physical Activity Challenge:

Exercise: Starting today, try engaging in physical activities you enjoy anytime you catch your narcissistic traits spinning the wheel. Whether it's yoga, lifting weights at the gym, walking, swimming, or dancing, get to it and notice how your mood shifts afterward. Write down two or three thoughts or emotions you experienced before, during, and after your activity. You can try different activities during different situations.

_____

_____

_____

_____

_____

_____

_____

_____

_____

_____

_____

Let's move on to another part that covers additional strategies that will help you in this journey.

Part V

Practical Strategies for Dealing with Narcissism

This is probably the main and most important part of this guide, as it provides you with strategies, tips, habits, tools, and secrets that will build up on the emotional intelligence and empathy you've learned in the previous part to help you leave narcissism behind for good!

Let's start with boosting your self-esteem.

Chapter 7: Building Genuine Self-Esteem

Would you say you have low or high self-esteem?

I ask this question because it is widely believed that narcissists have low self-esteem. But to the contrary, according to psychologists'[10] evaluations, narcissists have "high self-esteem." However, it is ***fragile***; that is probably why you likely do not feel secure about yourself and hence rely on self-deception and external validation.

This chapter provides tips on how to build genuine self-esteem. You will learn how to have a secure sense of worth and realize that the only validation you need and that matters the most comes from within.

Let's get started!

Recognize and Accept Your True Self

The first step in building genuine self-esteem is recognizing and accepting who you truly are, which includes both your strengths and weaknesses.

---

[10] https://www.ncbi.nlm.nih.gov/pmc/articles/PMC6070240/

Your current idea of who you are is probably led by the need for external validation, which you need to let go of. Instead, focus on acknowledging your authentic self, embracing your unique qualities, and understanding that your value and worth come from within.

To start, take time for *self-reflection*. Recognize your genuine strengths and the areas you may need improvement. As you do this, remember that everyone has flaws and that they do not diminish anyone's worth; they make us unique. When you accept both your beautiful and not-so-beautiful qualities, you allow yourself to appreciate your individuality and recognize areas you can work on to become better.

This acceptance promotes a sense of self-worth that does not depend on other people's opinions but yours. You become less dependent on constant praise and others' validation and more resilient to criticism. This helps you build a solid foundation for genuine self-esteem, enabling you to live a more fulfilling and authentic life.

Set Realistic Goals

Your self-esteem gets messed up every time you put yourself up for unrealistic goals (which happens a lot because you likely set most of your goals with the thoughts "what will so and so think"), and so, it is essential to ensure all your goals are realistic and attainable to avoid this. Be intentional about making goals that align with your values and interests instead of those aimed solely at gaining external approval. This is important because when you pursue what truly matters to you, your goals become more meaningful and fulfilling.

So, what really matters to you? Is it forming genuine connections, becoming more honest, being on good terms with your family, or starting your own business? Whatever your goals are, write them down.

After that, break these larger goals into smaller, manageable steps. Doing this helps make your goals less overwhelming and allows you to track your progress more effectively. Also, when you attain these smaller goals that lead to the success of the main goals, you get a sense of accomplishment, which helps boost your confidence and reinforce your underlying worth.

To help you stay motivated and keep a positive mindset towards your dreams, goals, and desires, celebrate your achievements, no matter how minor they may seem. Keep in mind that self-esteem is built through consistent, gradual steps rather than overnight success, so recognizing your progress goes a long way.

Engage in Activities You Enjoy

Participate in <u>hobbies</u>[11] and activities that you genuinely enjoy and that bring you joy and fulfillment. Whether reading, singing, cooking, or going for a nature walk, engaging in these activities helps you connect with your true self, allowing you to get satisfaction from your own experiences instead of relying on external validation. When you make it your habit to do what you love, you create moments of joy and contentment that boost your sense of worth.

These activities also allow you to build and refine talents and skills, which further help build your self-esteem. Whether it's painting, playing a musical instrument, gardening, or engaging in sports, the sense of accomplishment and improvement you experience can boost your confidence and self-worth.

Besides, doing what you love and enjoy helps relieve stress and fosters a sense of well-being. It gives you a break from life's pressure and allows you to focus on personal enjoyment and growth.

---

[11] https://medium.com/@adegustikumbara/boosting-confidence-self-esteem-how-hobbies-make-a-difference-d62f8e9ac2aa

Regularly participating in fulfilling activities nurtures a healthier, more positive self-image and develops a deeper appreciation for your unique abilities and interests.

Develop a Positive Self-Talk

Your traits can cause you to entertain and engage in negative self-talk more often, negatively affecting your self-esteem. Therefore, challenge any negative self-talk and replace it with positive affirmations to build genuine self-esteem. Whenever you catch yourself thinking about perceived shortcomings or negative thoughts about yourself, counter that by reminding yourself of your strengths and achievements. This helps build a more balanced and encouraging view of yourself.

For this strategy to be effective, you must actively recognize and dispute self-critical thoughts. For example, if you are doing a challenging work project and find yourself thinking, "I will never get this right. My career is doomed," pause and replace those self-limiting thoughts with more affirming and supportive ones such as, "I have all the resources and help I need to do this project, learn, and grow."

Also, from time to time, reflect on and recognize your capabilities and successes, no matter how small they may seem. This will help cultivate self-confidence and self-acceptance, weakening the power of self-doubt and criticism.

By consistently having more positive self-talk, you can transform your internal narrative. This helps boost your self-esteem and also promotes a healthier, more resilient approach to challenges and setbacks, encouraging a more optimistic outlook on life and strengthening your value and belief in yourself.

Give Back to Others

When you take part in acts of kindness and service[12], you shift your focus from seeking validation to contributing positively to others' lives. Volunteering or helping those in need gives you a sense of purpose and fulfillment that enhances your self-esteem. Setting time and putting in effort to support others allows you to experience the joy and satisfaction that comes from making a meaningful difference and connections.

Giving back to others also helps promote empathy and connection, which are crucial in counteracting narcissistic tendencies. You get to understand and respond to the needs of others, which enables you to develop a greater appreciation for different experiences and perspectives. This

---

[12] https://www.mayoclinichealthsystem.org/hometown-health/speaking-of-health/3-health-benefits-of-volunteering

not only builds emotional intelligence but also strengthens your relationships and social bonds.

Moreover, helping others allows you to realize that your value extends beyond recognition and personal achievements. It emphasizes the importance of community and compassion, which, in return, reminds you that true self-worth is found in the positive impact you make on the world around you. By regularly engaging in acts of kindness, you become more selfless, improving both your own well-being and the lives of others.

Cultivate Healthy Relationships

You probably keep people around even though you know they are taking advantage of you and do not have your best interest at heart because your ego feeds on the attention, validation, and praise you get from them. However, it is time to let them all go. Instead, aim to surround yourself with people who support and value you for who you are, not just for what you can do for them. Building healthy, reciprocal relationships based on mutual respect and understanding is essential for building genuine self-esteem[13]. These

---

[13] https://www.apa.org/news/press/releases/2019/09/relationships-self-esteem

relationships give you a sense of acceptance and belonging, which help remind you of your value.

But how do you build healthy relationships?

Some of the qualities that will help you form and maintain healthy relationships include trust, empathy, and honest and open communication, among other traits. With these qualities in your relationships, you will feel more comfortable being your true self. You will also be able to respect and support each other, creating healthy bonds that help boost your self-esteem and overall well-being.

Additionally, you will be open to receiving constructive feedback and different perspectives that can help you grow and develop. The mutual support and encouragement you give each other will help you recognize your strengths and the areas you need to improve without feeling criticized or devalued.

These benefits of healthy relationships help boost your self-esteem and allow you to create meaningful connections with common interests, giving your life balance and a sense of purpose.

Embrace a Growth Mindset

What is a growth mindset?

In simple words, a growth mindset is all about being open to learning from your experiences, even negative ones, instead of striving for perfection in every situation. Instead of believing that challenges and failures reflect your worth, <u>this mindset</u>[14] encourages you to view them as opportunities for improvement and growth. When you adopt a growth mindset, you become more resilient to different circumstances and adaptable to new opportunities in life, allowing you to accomplish a lot and impacting your sense of competence and self-worth.

In life, expect setbacks, failures, and challenges because they are inevitable. And when you experience them, try to see them as learning opportunities. When or if you make a mistake, instead of being discouraged and giving up on yourself, use the experience and lessons from the situation to improve your skills and knowledge.

With this mindset, you do not focus on the negative or unfavorable outcomes in different situations. Instead, you

---

[14]   <u>https://medium.com/big-self-society/the-growth-mindset-carol-dweck-on-how-our-self-beliefs-shape-us-5155be5ddd05</u>

will begin to appreciate the effort you put in and the lessons learnt. This will allow you to develop self-confidence based on your determination and development. You will have a more positive approach to life, boosting your self-esteem and enhancing your ability to achieve personal and professional growth.

Be Self-Compassionate

Do you remember what we said self-compassion is about in the previous chapter? Well, it involves treating yourself with the same kindness and understanding that you would offer a friend. When you make mistakes or face challenges, you likely criticize yourself, which is detrimental to your self-esteem. But cut yourself some slack; we all make mistakes and experience challenges; the best thing to do is to be kind and gentle with yourself.

So, recognize your own suffering, offer yourself comfort, and always remember that imperfection is a shared aspect of life. During failures or difficulties, allow yourself to feel hurt or disappointed, but keep in mind that the whole situation has nothing to do with your worth.

By being self-compassionate, you reduce feelings of inadequacy and kill the urge to be validated. When you make self-compassion your friend, you develop a positive image and become more resilient, helping you build a stronger foundation for genuine self-esteem. (We will discuss how to become self-compassionate in detail in another chapter).

Seek Professional Support

Building genuine self-esteem can be challenging, especially since your narcissist traits (which affect your self-esteem) are deeply rooted inside you, and it might take a while and effort to overcome them completely. So, when none of the tips discussed seem to work, do not hesitate to seek professional help.

Seeking the support of a therapist or counselor can provide you with personalized strategies and tools to work on your self-esteem. An expert will give you objective perspectives and professional advice for your unique needs, helping you understand and address the root causes of your narcissistic behaviors.

A therapist will help you understand and navigate your emotions and behaviors, leading to more profound and lasting changes. They will also help you develop healthier coping mechanisms to triggers and stress, improve your interpersonal skills, and boost self-compassion. Through professional help, you will better understand your thought patterns and get one-on-one guidance on replacing negative self-talk with positive ones.

Additionally, a professional will provide a safe space where you get to know your vulnerabilities and address any past experiences that may have led to your narcissistic tendencies. By addressing these issues with a qualified professional, you get to build stronger self-esteem and overcome narcissism altogether.

(We will discuss this point in another chapter.)

Worksheet:

Action 1: Strengths and Weaknesses Reflection:

Exercise: Take 15 minutes to reflect on your genuine strengths and areas you believe need some work. Write down three strengths you appreciate about yourself and two areas you need to improve. Also, consider how to use your strengths to overcome your shortcomings.

_____

_____

_____

_____

_____

_____

_____

_____

_____

_____

_____

_____

_____

Action 2: Goal Setting Exercise:

Exercise: Identify and write down one realistic and meaningful goal aligned with your values; it could concern any aspect of your life. Break it down into smaller steps by writing the first three actions you will take towards achieving it. How will achieving this goal contribute to your sense of self-worth? Write this down, too.

_____

_____

_____

_____

_____

_____

_____

_____

_____

_____

_____

_____

Action 3: Make a List of the Activities Your Enjoy:

Exercise: Write down five or more activities that bring you joy and fulfillment. Choose one activity to engage in this week, and at the end of the week, reflect on and describe how this activity makes you feel and how it aligns with your authentic self.

_____

_____

_____

_____

_____

_____

_____

_____

_____

_____

Action 4: Have Positive Affirmations for your Self-Esteem:

Exercise: Before, you created a mantra that promoted kindness, but now, have one or two that boost your self-esteem. Write them down and repeat them to yourself daily for the next week. Notice how they influence your mindset and self-perception.

_____

_____

_____

_____

_____

_____

_____

_____

_____

_____

_____

_____

Action 5: Acts of Kindness Plan:

Exercise: Plan one act of service or kindness for someone else this month. Describe what you will do and how you expect it to impact both the recipient and yourself.

_____

_____

_____

_____

_____

_____

_____

_____

_____

_____

_____

Action 6: Growth Mindset Reflection:

Exercise: Think of a recent setback or challenge you faced. Write about the lessons you learned from this experience and how you can apply them to future situations.

_____

_____

_____

_____

_____

_____

_____

_____

_____

_____

_____

_____

Action 7: Seeking Professional Help:

Exercise: Reflect on whether you feel you could benefit from professional support in building your self-esteem. If yes, outline the steps you can take this month to seek guidance from a therapist or counselor. If you don't know where to begin with this, do not worry; we will discuss professional help in the last chapter. But sure to determine if you need to work with an expert.

_____

_____

_____

_____

_____

_____

_____

_____

_____

_____

_____

_____

By implementing these strategies and exercises, you can build genuine self-esteem rooted in self-acceptance, compassion, and personal growth. This foundation of true self-worth will help you overcome narcissistic tendencies and lead to healthier, more fulfilling relationships with yourself and others.

Let's get to the next chapter and discuss how to set healthy boundaries as a strategy to stop narcissistic behaviors.

Chapter 8: Setting Healthy Boundaries

For any relationship to be successful and healthy, there must be boundaries. For now, you are aware that this hasn't been happening in your relationships, and that is why most if not all, tend to end or have unending conflicts. But the good news is, just like anyone, you can learn this essential quality in life so that your relationships can be healthy and grow into beautiful connections that make you happier.

Let's look at the different ways that have proven effective in helping set healthy boundaries:

Understand the Importance of Boundaries

If you ask anyone who is in a healthy relationship, especially romantic or sexual ones, they will tell you that you must understand and respect each other's boundaries[15] for any relationship to prosper.

But why?

---

[15] https://safehelpline.org/boundaries-and-healthy-relationships#:~:text=Healthy%20relationships%20are%20built%20on,to%20sexual%20or%20romantic%20partners.

To begin with, when you set boundaries, you **form the foundation for respect and balance** in your personal and professional relationships. Healthy boundaries help you realize where you draw the line and where the other person's is. Understanding and respecting this helps both parties feel respected and safe, which is what everyone is always looking for in every relationship.

Other benefits you will get from having healthy boundaries include:

- Your self-respect will increase because you won't just be respecting the other person's boundaries but yours too, which helps boost your sense of self-worth.

- With clear boundaries, you won't have to overextend yourself; hence, you won't have to deal with the stress and resentment that come from having conflicts that would otherwise not have happened had you set healthy boundaries.

- When you protect your personal space and time, you experience improved mental health and overall well-being.

- Also, setting healthy boundaries helps make your relationships healthier, increasing their chances of growing and reaching heights you never thought possible.

Boundaries are not barriers. They are essential to help avoid overstepping each other's limits, which is a main cause of conflicts and resentment. Do you want relationships where you respect yourself and others and where you can trust and find security? Well, you have to start setting your boundaries as early as now, which takes us to the next step.

Identify Your Boundaries

What do you like, and what do you not like? What doesn't sit well with you?

To know your boundaries, you must do some self-reflection. When you think about your past interactions, can you identify scenarios where you felt uncomfortable, overstepped others' limits, or allowed others to overstep yours? Think of the behaviors you consider acceptable and those you don't.

Also, think of times when you felt violated, resentful, and stressed and what triggered these feelings. Knowing these triggers can help you understand your limits more clearly. So, ask yourself what you need to feel safe and respected in various relationships such as family, work, romantic, and social. Realizing this will help you set boundaries that provide for your needs and protect your values.

Respect Others' Boundaries

As much as you would like your boundaries to be respected, so do others. So, learn the other person's boundaries to create balance in your relationships.

Start by being intentional to recognize and understand their verbal and non-verbal cues. When someone tells you they don't like something you do or say to them, acknowledge it and make the necessary change. For instance, if your partner tells you not to disturb or distract them during certain hours because they are working on a certain project, honor that request to show you value their needs.

When you respect their boundaries, it shows that you are understanding and empathetic, and this encourages them to respect your boundaries, too. This, in turn, boosts trust and helps minimize conflicts.

So, accept that we all have different limits, and what might be okay with you might not be okay with someone else. Do this in all your relationships and watch as they all flourish.

Communicate Clearly

You have to be <u>assertive</u>[16] and clear about your limits so that the other person can understand them. Therefore, be direct and specific when expressing your boundaries. For instance, instead of saying, "I need space," you will be better understood if you say, "I need 30 minutes of quiet time after work to relax and unwind." This way, the other person will not misunderstand you, and you won't be left feeling frustrated.

However, how you phrase your boundaries is important because the other person can easily feel criticized and blamed. To avoid this and still be able to communicate your needs, use "I" statements. For example, this statement, "I feel overwhelmed when there is constant noise, and I need some quiet time to recharge," will be received more than if you included a "you" in it.

Also, keep your tone respectful and calm to receive a receptive response. Avoid addressing issues that test your

---

[16] https://studentaffairs.stanford.edu/how-life-treeting-you-importance-of-boundaries#:~:text=Ideally%2C%20boundaries%20are%20communicated%20kindly,most%20helpful%20when%20communicating%20boundaries.

limits when your emotions are all over the place. Instead, take some time to calm down and deal with them when everyone can have a constructive conversation.

Learn to Say No

It is hard to say no[17], especially to the people we love, but for the boundaries you've set to be effective, you must learn how to. Say no to unreasonable requests or demands that do not align with your values and beliefs, as that is a way of protecting your well-being and respecting your limits.

You have the right to put your needs first, and no one should make you feel guilty about it. It's not selfish at all; it is essential for you to set and maintain healthy boundaries.

So, how do you say no?

Say no in a polite but firm way. For example, if your colleague wants you to help them with a certain project but you are not in a position to do so, you can say, "I understand where you are coming from, but I cannot take on this task right now." This shows that you recognize what they are asking of you but also communicates that you are unable to comply.

---

[17] https://fearlessliving.org/how-to-say-no-to-the-people-you-love/

When you say no when you need to, you become more confident in yourself and strengthen your boundaries. With practice, turning down requests that do not align with your capacity or value becomes easier, leading to more balanced and respectful relationships.

Be Consistent

You see, you can't tell someone that cheating is a deal breaker for you but go ahead and cheat on them. That gives the relationship an inconsistent vibe, leading to frustration, disrespect, and confusion for you and the other person.

So, you need to stand firm on your boundaries for them to be effective. Yes, sometimes it will get challenging, but always remember what you gain from being consistent with your boundaries.

Always refer to the benefits of setting boundaries (discussed earlier) whenever you need motivation, feel like giving up on your boundaries, or feel guilty for having them. Remember, maintaining your boundaries is a form of self-respect and teaches others how to treat you.

However, this does not mean you have to be rigid. Yes, you can reevaluate and change your boundaries when you need to, but ensure to communicate and stick to them.

Reflect and Adjust

From time to time, reflect and assess if your set boundaries are effective. Are they being respected and protecting your mental and emotional well-being? Also, do you feel some limits are being overlooked or tested frequently?

If you notice some boundaries that are not being respected, try to find out why. Is it that you are not communicating them clearly, or are you not being consistent enough? Or is it that the other person simply doesn't care about your values and feelings, and the relationship has run its course?

Finding the answers to these questions will help you know your next step.

However, make sure to be flexible with your boundaries. Life is constantly changing, and so are the dynamics of different relationships. Therefore, be open and willing to adjust your boundaries as necessary to ensure they are relevant and effective.

For instance, if you need 30 minutes a day by yourself at the end of the day to unwind and relax, but that doesn't seem to work anymore, you can replace it with 30 minutes of quality time with your daughter or son or any important person before bed.

When you do this, you ensure that your boundaries are serving you well.

Worksheet:

Action 1: Reflect on Your Boundary Needs:

Exercise: Take time to journal about situations in your life where you have felt taken advantage of or uncomfortable. Identify three specific instances and write down what boundaries you wish you had set in those moments. How would setting these boundaries have changed the outcome?

_____

_____

_____

_____

_____

_____

_____

_____

_____

_____

_____

_____

_____

_____

Action 2: Boundary Setting Practice:

Exercise: Choose one or several relationships in your life in which you feel boundaries are needed but haven't been established. Write down the specific boundaries you want to set in this/these relationship/s. Write how these boundaries will benefit both you and the other person.

_____

_____

_____

_____

_____

_____

_____

_____

_____

_____

_____

_____

Action 3: Role Play Communication:

Exercise: Think of someone who can help you practice asserting your boundaries through role play. It could be a trusted friend, colleague, or family member. Choose a scenario where you struggle to set boundaries (for example, saying no to additional work tasks or discussing personal time needs), and then practice communicating such boundaries. Remember to use "I" statements and maintain a calm, respectful tone.

_____

_____

_____

_____

_____

_____

_____

_____

_____

_____

_____

_____

Action 4: Create Your Boundary Statement:

Exercise: Craft a clear and assertive statement for one of your identified boundaries. Practice saying this statement aloud until you feel comfortable with it, then move to the next.

_____

_____

_____

Action 5: Saying "No" Exercise:

Exercise: Practice saying no to a request that doesn't align with your values or capacity. Choose a small request you would normally agree to out of guilt or obligation. How does saying no to something that doesn't fit your values make you feel?

_____

_____

_____

Action 6: Evaluate Boundary Effectiveness:

Exercise: Reflect on one boundary you have recently set. Has it been respected? How has it impacted your relationship and well-being? If adjustments are needed, brainstorm one adjustment you can make to strengthen this boundary.

_____

_____

_____

_____

_____

_____

_____

_____

_____

_____

Action 7: Weekly Boundary Check-in:

Exercise: Dedicate some time each week to review your boundaries in different relationships. Note any instances where your boundaries were tested or where you felt the need to reinforce them. Adjust as necessary and celebrate moments where your boundaries were respected during the week.

_____

_____

_____

_____

_____

_____

_____

_____

_____

_____

_____

_____

Now that you know how to set healthy boundaries, let's get to the next chapter, where we will discuss how to build resilience and coping skills to help you stay firm on your journey to leaving narcissist traits behind!

Chapter 9: Building Resilience and Coping Skills

I won't lie to you; unlearning some of the behaviors, habits, or traits you've had and known for a long time <u>is not easy</u>[18], and without resilience and coping skills, you might not succeed.

In simple terms, resilience is the ability to face and overcome setbacks and challenges. Coping skills are the tools you need to help deal with different emotions in a healthy way. These two skills will help manage your narcissistic traits and also lead to personal and professional growth.

So, let's find out how to develop each:

Understanding and Building Resilience

In your journey to becoming better and improving your life, you will face challenges, and how you face them determines whether you will put an end to narcissism or not. Resilience is the ability to pick yourself up after adversity, adapt to challenges, and keep rooting for yourself even when the odds are against you.

---

[18] https://www.psychologytoday.com/au/blog/the-craving-mind/201908/the-science-behind-bad-habits-and-how-break-them

For you, as a person trying to become better and leave the current toxic traits behind, building resilience entails *learning to handle criticism, failure, and disappointment without resorting to defensive or aggressive behaviors.* It involves learning better ways to respond to stress and challenges without having to worry about what others will think of you.

So, to become more resilient:

View Challenges as Learning Opportunities

You need to know that challenges are there to help us learn and improve. Even when you talk to your role model or listen to an inspiring story from someone thriving in life, they will tell you that <u>there is no growth or change without challenges.</u>[19]

So, starting today, when you face challenges, don't see them as threats sent to destroy your self-worth and turn to narcissistic behaviors as your coping mechanism. Do not give up and let the negative thoughts that make you believe that you are not good enough take charge, hence the need to seek others' validation. Instead, accept them as learning

---

[19]   https://authorbeckyjohnen.wordpress.com/2015/07/27/you-cant-spell-challenge-without-change/

opportunities: you can always learn something from every situation.

For example, suppose you make a mistake during a presentation at work, and your colleague points it out. In this case, instead of becoming defensive or angry or holding a grudge against them, take a step back, reflect on everything, and consider the lesson you get from the situation. Ask yourself questions like, "What led to the mistake?" or "How can I prepare better next time to avoid similar errors?"

When you pay attention to the lesson instead of the perceived failure, you change the unfavorable experience into a valuable learning opportunity. This changes how you view positive criticism and helps you develop a growth mindset.

Use this approach in different aspects of your life. Your resilience will grow, and you will be able to handle whatever life throws your way without hurting yourself and others emotionally and mentally.

You won't feel the need to blame others because you understand that you need both positive and negative experiences to become stronger and keep growing.

Develop a Growth Mindset

We saw that a growth mindset helps build self-esteem, but there is more to it; it <u>helps build resilience</u>[20], too. With this mindset, you are willing to learn and develop. You do not seek to be perfect but better because you know that abilities and intelligence can be developed through effort and practice.

To develop a growth mindset that will help you handle challenges and become resilient as you strive to learn new behaviors:

- *Challenge Yourself:* Take on tasks or goals outside your comfort zone to develop new skills and qualities, and do not let challenges discourage you. For example, if you've always had to have someone by your side whenever you go out because you love how much they praise you, challenge that by trying to go out more on your own and enjoying your own company.

- *Learn from Criticism:* Accept feedback gracefully and reflect on it to identify where and how to become better. When a friend or anyone tells you that they do not like it

---

[20]   <u>https://www.thebci.org/news/using-a-growth-mindset-to-build-resilience.html</u>

when you try to control their decisions, accept that and work on it.

- *Focus on Effort, Not Talent*: Hard work pays, so put in the effort, whether in your career or studies, and be persistent. Don't let anything make you believe that you can never prosper in what you dream of without talent. Remember, practice makes perfect; you just have to be willing to learn.

- *Celebrate Progress:* When you notice a positive change in your behavior, celebrate and be proud of yourself. It could be that you showed empathy to a stranger on your way home or had a difficult conversation with your partner without blaming each other. But whatever it is that contributes to your progress, small or big, celebrate it.

- *Stay Curious:* Maintain a sense of curiosity and a desire to explore new ideas and perspectives. Also, engage in continuous learning through reading, courses, and other educational activities.

- *Surround yourself with Growth-Oriented People:* The company you keep has the power to influence your mindset, so spend time with people who encourage and support your growth. Learn from their experiences and insights, and be willing to share yours.

Self-Reflect

Regularly, take some time and reflect on whether your behaviors associated with narcissistic tendencies have changed or not. Do you still get triggered by the things that once caused you to fall into the narcissism trap?

Since you are actively trying to cut narcissism from the room, you must be intentional and monitor your progress through self-reflection. For example, at the end of the week, you could sit by yourself and reflect on different situations.

How did you react when your partner said no to you?

Did you get angry and aggressive, or did you try to understand them?

What about the time you received negative feedback on your project?

Did you welcome the constructive feedback with a growth mindset, or did you become defensive and blame your colleague?

Keep practicing self-reflection to learn your behavioral patterns. When do you consistently feel threatened? During which situations do you seem to crave approval and attention? Recognizing your patterns will help you realize which traits are improving and which ones you still need to work on.

Noticing the progress you've made in some areas will motivate you to keep going, and recognizing the negative traits that are present will help you focus on them, leading to improvement. Over time, you will be able to challenges and setbacks more constructively, not only the ones related to your narcissistic behaviors but <u>all aspects of your life</u>[21]. This will, in turn, make you more resilient.

Developing Coping Skills

Breaking patterns is not easy because they are rooted deep in our subconscious mind, and the mind doesn't like change. So, don't give in whenever you feel like respecting others' boundaries is just too much or when your mind tries to trick you into throwing empathy outside the window, which might happen often at the beginning of your journey. Instead, try these skills that will help you keep rooting for a better you, boosting your resilience and motivating you:

---

[21] https://medium.com/@XhoeVi/the-power-of-self-reflection-building-resilience-for-personal-growth-and-success-623ce5627e8a

Practice Mindfulness Meditation

Mindfulness meditation is a practice where you intentionally focus on the present moment and observe your thoughts and feelings without judgment. When you take a moment anytime you feel triggered to do this, you increase your self-awareness and get to regulate your emotions. This allows you to respond or address the situation more thoughtfully rather. You won't act impulsively.

So, make meditation your go-to friend anytime you feel triggered. Do you remember the meditation steps we discussed earlier? Add them to your routine if you haven't yet or if you started and stopped somewhere along the way.

Allow this practice to help you learn how to recognize and manage your emotional triggers, reducing the need for external validation and aggressive responses. Practicing mindfulness meditation frequently or as needed will lead to greater emotional stability[22] and a positive approach to life, helping you develop healthier relationships and boost your sense of self-worth.

---

[22]

https://www.betterup.com/blog/triggers#:~:text=Mindfulness%20allows%20you%20to%20observe,stay%20present%20in%20the%20moment.

The good thing about this practice is that it will not only calm and bring your mind to the moment but will also boost empathy, which you must have to overcome narcissism.

Try Deep Breathing Exercises

Sometimes, all you may need is a few deep breaths for a situation to stop messing up with your emotions and mood.

Taking deep breaths helps calm your nervous system and reduce stress, which allows you to manage emotions better. When you catch yourself feeling overwhelmed or when something triggers you, practice deep breathing exercises to help reduce stress[23] and prevent impulsive, defensive reactions typical of narcissistic tendencies.

An easy and effective deep breathing exercise is the 4-7-8 technique. To do this, take a deep 4-second breath through the nose, hold it for 7 seconds, then breathe out through the mouth for 8 seconds. Repeat for a few minutes and notice how your mind calms down and your body feels lighter.

Make this one of your favorite coping skills anytime your thoughts and feelings become so much that you want to blame someone or say something demeaning. In return, you

---

[23]   https://www.healthline.com/health/diaphragmatic-breathing#other-exercises

will be able to process and understand your emotions and choose more thoughtful, empathetic reactions. Your emotional resilience will become better day after day, making it easier to navigate the challenges you meet on the way.

Journal

If you still don't have a journal, get one as soon as possible. Thanks to technology, there are several journaling apps for phones and computers, but many say that they find the traditional book and pen journaling technique more effective; you can always try the one that works best for you.

In this journal, regularly write about your thoughts and emotions. For example, if you felt insulted by a colleague's comment or feedback at work, writing about the situation, your experience, and your response can help you understand why you felt hurt and how to respond more constructively in the future. In other words, journaling allows you to reflect on your behavior, recognize areas for improvement, and develop healthier responses.

Also, journaling provides a safe space to express your feelings without judgment, which can kill the need to seek external praise or validation. With time, this coping skill will help build your emotional intelligence. You will gradually learn to reshape your mindset to one that leaves the negative traits behind and adopts healthier ones, such as empathy, forgiveness, and open communication.

Speaking of empathy...

Continue Practicing Empathy

We dedicated a whole chapter to why empathy is important and how to be more empathetic so we won't get to it in deals. But just to remind you, empathy will help change your self-centered way of thinking to one that cares about other people's feelings and ideas. This is a very effective method of overcoming narcissism and coping with different situations, and it has the ability to make you more resilient.

Therefore, remember to take part in activities that help you understand and share the feelings of others. Whether volunteering for community service, spending time listening to others' experiences without interrupting, or helping a stranger in need, a little act of kindness goes a long way for you and others.

Practice Cognitive Restructuring

Cognitive restructuring[24] refers to identifying and challenging irrational or harmful thoughts as they happen and replacing them with more rational and beneficial ones. Negative or perfectionist thoughts bring no good to your life, so letting them go and entertaining constructive ones is the only best option for you and those around you.

So, be intentional in adopting a positive thought pattern. For instance, if you often think, "I am a bad person for cutting off so-and-so," you can replace this thought with, "It's okay to let go of friends and associates who trigger negative behaviors, emotions, or thoughts."

But where do you begin?

Refer to your journal to recognize situations that trigger negative thoughts, then look for evidence for and against these beliefs. Are these beliefs or thoughts that make you believe you need validation real? Or are they false distortions that exist only in your mind? It's probably the latter, right?

Once you have facts tabled out, you will be more open to practicing all the strategies we've discussed and are yet to,

---

[24] https://www.sciencedirect.com/topics/psychology/cognitive-restructuring

which will help boost your self-image. You will also become better at regulating your emotions. This is because you now know that the beliefs that trigger or used to trigger you are from distorted thinking, which you have replaced or are learning to replace with rational and constructive ones.

Build a Support Network

We all need someone we can count on, so having a support system is a crucial coping skill. It could be anyone you trust, such as your friend, family, colleague, mentor, therapist, or lover. Whoever they are, they can encourage you to keep putting in the work, give you honest feedback on your progress, and be your accountability partner/s.

Also, they can help you gain different perspectives in different situations and provide emotional support in the face of challenges. These are essential for personal growth and self-improvement.

If you do not have a support network, actively seek out to create one with empathetic and understanding people. Join groups or communities that share your interests or values, as this leads to relationships with mutual respect rather than superficial admiration.

Call your mentor or book an extra appointment with your therapist whenever you need someone to talk to. Reach out to family or long-lost friends to mend things and be there for each other.

Keeping your support system close reduces feelings of isolation and decreases the need for constant validation. You create an environment that encourages positive change and emotional resilience, which help you develop healthier relationships and a stronger, more grounded identity.

But, keep in mind that for this to be effective, you must have the same beliefs, values, and interests as the people you spend time with and turn to for a leaning shoulder; do not expect someone with narcissist traits but is unwilling to become better to help you do so, they will definitely hold you back.

Practice Self-compassion

We won't discuss self-compassion much here because that's our next chapter. But as mentioned earlier, self-compassion involves treating yourself with kindness and understanding, especially when you face setbacks or make mistakes.

You see the advice and kindness you would give a loved one who is having a hard time; take it when you start criticizing yourself for not being perfect. Remember, we are all flawed, and there is no such thing as perfection.

When you are more understanding of your emotions and thoughts, especially the negative or unhealthy ones, you are better placed to address and replace them instead of suppressing them.

Worksheet:

Action 1: Challenge Identification Exercise:

Exercise: Think about any recent challenge or setback you faced. Write down how you initially reacted to this situation. Did any of these reactions involve aggressive or defensive behaviors? Reflect on how these reactions affected the outcome of the situation and how you could have responded differently.

_____

_____

_____

_____

_____

_____

_____

_____

_____

_____

_____

Action 2: Growth Mindset Journaling:

Exercise: Start a growth mindset journal. Each day, write down one challenge you faced and how you approached it with a growth mindset. For example, if you received constructive criticism, reflect on how you accepted it and what you learned from the feedback. Also, reward your efforts in embracing challenges as opportunities for growth.

_____

_____

_____

_____

_____

_____

_____

_____

_____

_____

_____

Action 3: Support System Evaluation:

Exercise: Evaluate your current support system. List one or two people in your life whom you trust to provide honest feedback and emotional support. Consider reaching out to one of them this week to discuss one challenge you have been facing. Note down their insights and how their support impacted your resilience.

_____

_____

_____

_____

_____

_____

_____

_____

_____

_____

_____

_____

Action 4: Cognitive Restructuring Practice:

Exercise: Identify one recurring negative thought pattern related to your self-worth or abilities. Use a journal or notes app to write down this negative thought whenever it arises. Next to it, challenge it with rational, positive statements. Track your progress in replacing negative thoughts with more constructive beliefs.

Action 5: Empathy Building Exercise:

Exercise: Decide on one activity to practice empathy this week. It could be volunteering, donating to the less fortunate, or having a heartfelt conversation with a friend. Reflect on how this experience deepened your understanding of others' emotions and perspectives.

_____

_____

_____

With that covered, let's get to the next chapter and learn how to cultivate compassion for yourself and others, as it evidently is an essential tool for overcoming narcissistic behavior.

Chapter 10: Developing Self-Compassion and Altruism

Let's begin this chapter by testing your progress. Do you know that you are likely self-centered? I know that's harsh of me to say, but I am not telling you this to hurt you. As constructive feedback, and if you've been practicing what we've been learning, you know it is better to welcome criticism.

The problem with this trait is that it benefits no one, not you or others. It makes you focus on yourself so much that you want to be perfect in everything and tend to project the same image on others, and this leads to all the character traits of narcissism we discussed. But remember, there is no such thing as perfection.

So, to get rid of self-centredness, you must develop self-compassion and altruism. These two qualities will help change how you view yourself and others. You will[25] develop a more balanced and empathetic approach toward yourself and others, no matter what happens in life.

---

[25] https://www.mindful.org/the-transformative-effects-of-mindful-self-compassion/#:~:text=An%20explosion%20of%20research%20into,and%20less%20anxiety%20and%20depression.

You will become happier, feel more motivated, create better relationships, find more satisfaction in your authentic life, become less depressed and anxious about your life, boost your resilience, and improve your mental and physical health.

Self-compassion is treating yourself with kindness and understanding, especially during setbacks or when you make mistakes. Altruism, on the other hand, is caring for others selflessly. Both self-compassion and altruism help boost a sense of purpose and fulfillment, which overpowers your need to care only for yourself.

Together, they enable you to create healthier relationships and a more grounded, empathetic self-image. Embracing these qualities empowers you to keep journeying away from narcissistic tendencies.

How to Develop Self-Compassion

To become more self-compassionate:

Acknowledge Your Flaws and Mistakes

We all make mistakes, including you, which is okay; they are part of our learning and growth journey. So, do not criticize yourself the next time you mess up or fail. Do not say anything negative to yourself.

Understand that anyone under the same circumstances would have made the same or similar mistake, and there is no need to beat yourself up about it.

What you can do is try to learn the lessons the experience seeks to teach you and move on. Be kind to yourself and focus on what you can do to improve in the future.

For instance, if you miss a deadline, resist the urge to berate yourself. Instead, accept that mistakes do happen and one has just happened. Focus on what you can learn from the experience and how you can do better next time.

Do you need to manage your time better?

Do you need to divide the task into smaller tasks so it is not overwhelming?

Do you need to learn a new skill to be better prepared?

When you accept your flaws and mistakes, you let go of the need for perfection and adopt a mindset that is willing to learn, let go, and grow. Forgive yourself every time you fail and keep trying different approaches; you will eventually succeed, boosting your self-esteem, self-confidence, and self-image so that you won't need anyone's validation anymore. Additionally, you won't feel the need to criticize yourself anymore.

Use Positive Affirmations

We are what we feed our minds with. So, if you keep telling yourself, "I have to be perfect in this and this," "I don't deserve them; they are too good for me," or "I am not worth it," you will keep believing this and will always run to your narcissist traits for comfort and "safety."

To avoid letting negative thoughts in, be intentional in affirming yourself as often as possible. It has been proven that affirmations impact your life in many ways,[26] including boosting your self-compassion.

You can create some time in your routine to say positive affirmations to yourself in the morning or at the end of the day. Also, during the day, when you catch yourself having a negative self-thought, pause for a second and replace it with a positive one.

Simple statements such as, "I am worthy of love and respect," or "I am doing my best, and that's enough" can help reframe your inner dialogue, making it more supportive and kind.

---

[26]   https://www.psychologytoday.com/us/blog/the-age-of-overindulgence/202307/the-science-behind-self-affirmations#:~:text=Affirmations%20are%20short%20statements%20that,in%20a%20variety%20of%20ways.

Making this a habit will feed your mind with positive and kind thoughts that will change your self-image and mindset.

Practice Mindfulness

Remember to include mindfulness in everything you do. Try as much as possible to live in the moment.

But how do you do this?

Here is an example to help you understand what including mindfulness in your life means.

If you are working on a research project, stop worrying about the fight you had with your spouse in the morning. Yes, the thoughts will cross your mind from time to time, but acknowledge them and, without judgment, bring your attention back to the project.

Or,

If you are preparing dinner, pay attention to how the water feels on your hands when you wash an ingredient or how the aroma changes with every step. Yes, you might worry about where to get your rent money or more capital for your business but do not engage those thoughts. Just keep bringing your attention back to the food you are making and how the experience makes you feel.

When you practice mindfulness, you do not have time to worry or criticize yourself. This helps create a mindset that is willing to experience and learn, and so you will find it easy to implement the different strategies for putting an end to narcissism, self-compassion included.

How to Develop Altruism

Now that you know how to be kind to yourself, it's time to help give this amazing trait some balance so you don't end up self-centered or insensitive. This can be achieved through altruism, which we said is the ability to care for others and extend kindness genuinely:

Perform Random Acts of Kindness

Small, spontaneous acts of kindness, such as gifting your spouse out of the blue, sharing an umbrella with a stranger on your way home, or helping your colleague with a project, can have a <u>breathtaking impact on others and you, too</u>. These acts help you focus from self-centered concerns to the well-being of those around you.

Whether it's offering a genuine compliment, offering to babysit your sibling's or friend's baby, or donating to charity, these actions will help you build a habit of thinking about and caring for others.

When or if someone comes to you because they are going through a tough time, offering them kind words can uplift their spirits and create a more positive environment. Also, donating to a cause that really touches your heart, even in small amounts, helps strengthen your value of generosity and community support.

As you continue practicing these random acts of kindness, they pay you back by helping change your mindset and behaviors for the better, as long as you do them with a pure heart. They help develop empathy, reduce narcissistic tendencies, and create a more fulfilling and connected way of interacting with the world around you.

Reflect on the Impact of Your Actions

After making acts of kindness to your friends, reflect on them from time to time. Think of the time you helped a stranger in need and how happy they were at that moment. Think of the time you complimented your friend and how that helped put a smile on their face.

Reflecting on the positive impact of your acts of compassion and generosity can motivate you to continue being selfless. This helps foster empathy, among other qualities that automatically replace narcissistic tendencies.

Join Supportive Communities

Actively seek to create relationships with people who value kindness and altruism. The company we keep can greatly influence our behavior[27], so if you spend more time with kind and generous people, you will find yourself becoming kind and generous, too.

So, join groups or communities that focus on giving back and supporting each other. Join local charity organizations, participate in community service clubs, or join online groups dedicated to volunteering and mutual support.

Joining such groups or communities will allow you to observe and learn from others who prioritize compassion and selflessness. They also offer a platform to share your experiences and receive encouragement and feedback.

Also, sharing the same spirit of giving and mutual aid with others helps shift your focus from self-centered concerns to the broader well-being of others. This will help you form new healthy relationships with shared interests and significantly impact your journey of becoming the best version of yourself.

---

[27] https://www.ncbi.nlm.nih.gov/pmc/articles/PMC7072047/

Worksheet:

Action 1: Self-Compassion Journaling:

Exercise: Have a journal dedicated to self-compassion. Each day, write down one mistake or flaw you've accepted about yourself without judgment. Reflect on how you responded to this flaw positively and what lessons you learned from embracing self-compassion. Share one compassionate statement you'd tell a friend in a similar situation.

Action 2: Mindful Living Exercise:

Exercise: Pick a daily activity to practice mindfulness. Whether having a meal, walking in the park, or washing dishes, focus all your attention and senses on the activity. When distracting thoughts arise, gently bring your attention back to the task at hand.

Note down the feelings or insights you get from this practice and how it influences your self-awareness.

_____

_____

_____

_____

_____

_____

_____

_____

_____

_____

_____

Action 3: Random Acts of Kindness Challenge:

Exercise: Challenge yourself to perform one random act of kindness each day for a week. You could send your partner some flowers, send a thoughtful message to a friend, or help a sibling with a chore. At the end of the day or week, think of how these acts made you feel and how they impacted others.

_____

_____

_____

_____

_____

_____

_____

_____

_____

_____

_____

Action 4: Community Engagement Reflection:

Exercise: Join a community or group that values altruism and kindness. Attend a meeting or participate in a volunteer event. Reflect on and write how being part of this community impacted your sense of purpose and connection with others. Discuss your experience with a friend or family member and think of ways to contribute further.

_____

_____

_____

_____

_____

_____

_____

_____

_____

_____

_____

Action 5: Gratitude Practice:

Exercise: End each day by writing down three or five things you are grateful for, focusing on moments of kindness or compassion you experienced or shared.

_____

_____

_____

_____

_____

_____

_____

_____

_____

_____

Moving on, let's get to another chapter and learn yet another effective tactic that will help leave NPD or associated traits behind.

Chapter 11: Embracing Vulnerability

One reason you show narcissistic traits is that you probably don't let yourself be vulnerable. You have a deep-seated fear of appearing weak or imperfect, and you have come to convince yourself that vulnerability is a weakness.

However, this couldn't be anywhere near the truth. Vulnerability is not a sign of weakness but strength and authenticity. One thing with humans is that we value authenticity, even though we might forget that vulnerability plays a big part in it. When you let yourself get vulnerable and show your true self, you are able to have genuine relationships and emotional intimacy. This openness <u>reduces your need to appear perfect</u>[28] and relieves the associated anxiety, creating a foundation for personal and even professional development.

This chapter will guide you through understanding and embracing vulnerability as a pathway to reducing narcissistic tendencies and fostering a more balanced, empathetic approach to life.

---

[28]   https://www.forbes.com/sites/danschawbel/2013/04/21/brene-brown-how-vulnerability-can-make-our-lives-better/

Understanding Vulnerability

Vulnerability entails being honest about your feelings, struggles, and imperfections. It means allowing others to see the real you, including your fears and weaknesses.

Yes, it does feel risky to trust others so much that you let them see the "not-so-strong or perfect" side of you, but vulnerability is an essential quality you need to nurture. Being vulnerable helps remind you and show others that it is okay to be imperfect. This increases understanding and mutual support and strengthens your bond with the world around you, leading to more authentic connections and reducing narcissistic traits.

Here is an example of how you can show vulnerability. Suppose you feel overwhelmed by a project at work. Instead of pretending that is fine, open up to a trusted colleague or even your partner about your struggles and feelings.

But why is vulnerability important?

The Benefits of Vulnerability

Deeper Connections

When you make sharing your truth with the people you trust part of your life, you will definitely have more <u>meaningful</u>

relationships[29] with stronger bonds. Opening up teaches people to trust you because you are brave and authentic enough to trust them with your fears, struggles, and challenges to begin with.

This creates a sense of closeness and mutual understanding that you cannot achieve if you keep your vulnerabilities to yourself.

There is a saying that goes, "A problem shared is a problem half-solved." Being open and honest with your struggles will not only boost your relationships but also lead to growth and change because you will gain a new perspective to deal with everything life throws at you. For instance, admitting to a friend that you're feeling insecure about a job interview can open up a dialogue where they share their own experiences and offer support.

Emotional Growth

Sharing your vulnerabilities can lead to significant personal growth, especially emotional. When you acknowledge your imperfections to yourself and others, you take the first step,

---

[29] https://www.verywellmind.com/why-vulnerability-in-relationships-is-so-important-5193728#:~:text=Vulnerability%20is%20an%20opportunity%20to,empathy%2C%20and%20builds%20stronger%20bonds.

understanding your emotions better, which then you can work through to deal with constructively, rather than letting them control you.

So, if you fear failure, share what you feel comfortable with, as long as it is the truth, to whoever you feel comfortable with. It could be your friend, relative, close family, or mentor. This takes the emotional burden off your shoulders and gives you fresh insights and strategies to overcome it, fostering self-improvement.

This emotional exploration and acceptance process allows you to build emotional intelligence that helps build resilience. As such, you will be better able to cope with future challenges, contributing to your overall personal development and emotional well-being.

Reduced Anxiety

Nothing can make you as tired as trying to live in a shell; you will attest to this after learning to be more vulnerable and make it a habit. Hiding your true self and constantly trying to appear perfect is exhausting and often leaves us feeling anxious. However, when you let others in on your weaknesses and struggles, you take the pressure of keeping up with lies and deceit off your shoulders, and suddenly, your life feels easier and more relaxed.

When you are vulnerable, you let go of the unrealistic expectations of perfection. This acceptance reduces the stress of maintaining a facade and allows you to experience life more genuinely. Over time, this openness brings peace of mind and soul into life and <u>boosts your mental health</u>[30], allowing you to meet your genuine self.

So, how can you practice vulnerability?

Steps to Embrace Vulnerability

They include:

Step 1: Acknowledge Your Fears

What are you afraid of? Is it failure, judgment, loneliness, rejection, or imperfection?

What makes you want to hide your true self?

The first step to becoming more vulnerable is recognizing your fears. Therefore, take some time to reflect on situations that trigger these fears and consider why they affect you so deeply.

---

[30] <u>https://www.ncbi.nlm.nih.gov/pmc/articles/PMC9521647/</u>

Is it that as a child, you were taught that imperfection is bad? Did you experience criticism every time you failed that you came to believe that failure is not good? Or do you have attachment issues that you fear being alone?

Identify your underlying fears and their root causes so that you know when to begin facing them. You do not have to avoid and deny them anymore because, at the end of the day, nothing good will come from it.

So, what is it that keeps you up at night?

Step 2: Share Your Feelings

After you recognize your fears, try sharing them, one at a time, with someone you trust and know will listen without judging you. It could be a close friend, family member, or therapist. Talk about the experiences that trigger your fears and emotions, which could be present or past.

Start small and gradually open up more as you become comfortable. For instance, if you were bullied at school when young because of your body size, size, or complexion, you can begin by sharing a minor concern or worry, for example, being honest about how you do not like being referred to in a certain way. As you build trust and confidence, you can move on to more significant issues, like some traumatic experiences you had concerning the same when growing up and how they made you feel.

This practice helps you become more accustomed to expressing vulnerability and strengthens your relationships. The supportive responses you receive from a caring and empathetic person make you feel that it's safe to be open, encouraging further emotional sharing and deeper connections.

Step 3: Accept Imperfection

You see the person you imagine to be perfect and probably look up to them because they seem to have it all together. Well, sorry to disappoint you. They are not as perfect as you imagine. They, too, have flaws and struggles and make mistakes.

And,

This doesn't mean that you should stop looking up to them; it means they are as human as anyone and are not perfect, and believing otherwise is just making life hard for no reason or reward. Therefore, you should let yourself be human and let go of the need to be perfect. Remind yourself that it's okay not to be perfect.[31]

When you make mistakes, accept them. When you fail, accept the outcome and lessons from the experience. When you feel afraid, accept and admit your feelings. Adopting this mindset can be liberating and reduces the pressure to maintain an unrealistic image of yourself. Embracing imperfection allows you to be more authentic and less guarded, creating a healthier and more honest relationship with yourself and those around you.

Step 4: Seek and Welcome Feedback

Can you say that you are an honest and open person? If you don't know, you can ask a trusted person to give you feedback on how you come across in interactions.

Looking for and accepting feedback will allow you to learn a thing or two about how you can be more open and genuine. For example, you might ask a colleague how you handled a recent meeting or ask a friend what they think of your communication style. They will provide constructive feedback that can highlight areas where you may be overly

---

[31]   https://medium.com/@mennovanderland/perfection-is-an-illusion-pursuing-it-is-a-recipe-for-unhappiness-1733c6197cb9

defensive or closed off and suggest what you could do to improve.

However, do not receive feedback and sit on it. Instead, accept it and work to make adjustments that foster greater openness and vulnerability. This will ultimately make you more authentic and build your vulnerability.

Step 5: Practice Empathy

Empathy can also help you become more vulnerable. Therefore, in every situation, especially those that bring out the other person's vulnerabilities, try to put yourself in their shoes and understand them. Doing this fosters empathy, making it easier for you to be vulnerable and compassionate towards them and yourself.

For instance, if a friend lost their loved one, empathize by considering how you would feel in their situation. This will allow you to connect with them on a deeper level and help you realize that vulnerability is a shared human experience.

Regularly practicing empathy will make you more comfortable sharing your own struggles and weaknesses, transform your relationships into more supportive ones, and foster a compassionate environment that encourages open and honest communication.

Step 6: Take Risks

Be brave enough to step out of your emotional comfort zone. Yes, there is comfort in knowing that no one knows your vulnerabilities because your chances of getting betrayed are low. But this doesn't help you feel or become any better; if anything, it leaves you feeling more overwhelmed, and you will find yourself displaying more narcissistic behaviors to help keep your true, vulnerable self hidden.

So, today, I want you to take a limp of faith, of course, with someone you trust and share something that has been bothering you. Don't think of the what-ifs: what if they laugh at me or don't get me? Do it for you; help yourself lift a burden off your heart and mind by expressing your feelings, asking for help, or admitting a mistake. These actions can help you grow more comfortable with vulnerability.

Start with small emotional risks, such as sharing a personal story with a friend, and gradually take on bigger challenges. For example, if you've been pretending that you are comfortable taking on all or most of the roles at home, you can be open about it and ask for help from your family.

Each time you take a risk and experience positive outcomes, your confidence in being vulnerable increases. Over time, these practices will help you embrace authenticity and vulnerability.

Overcoming the Fear of Judgment

Most of us are afraid of becoming vulnerable because we fear being judged, which is fueled by the belief that vulnerability is a sign of weakness. And so, every time one thinks of opening up, they get overpowered by intrusive thoughts such as, "What if they start seeing me differently?" or "What if they judge and laugh at me?"

The funny thing is, <u>according to Author and Professor Brené Brown</u>[32], even though you might view vulnerabilities as a negative trait, you likely find it admirable as a strength in others.

---

[32]

https://www.amazon.com/gp/product/1592408419?ie=UTF8&tag=greg 00scicen-

20&linkCode=as2&camp=1789&creative=9325&creativeASIN=15924084 19

Fortunately, you can overcome this fear and become more vulnerable through these simple ways:

- **Reframe Negative Thoughts:** Whenever you catch yourself having negative thoughts about your weaknesses, failures, or challenges, challenge those thoughts and replace them with positive affirmations. For example, instead of thinking, "I'm not good enough," remind yourself, "I am capable and worthy."

  Also, pay more attention to your strengths and achievements compared to your shortcomings. Consistently practicing this will help boost a positive self-image and shift your mindset from self-criticism to self-compassion, making it easier to be open and vulnerable.

- **Focus on Growth:** When we said focus on your strengths and achievements, we meant growth, too. We all are capable of learning and growing in our own ways, and that is a strength that is unique to everyone. So, instead of approaching your vulnerabilities as weaknesses, view them as opportunities. Every time you let someone in and open up to them, you gain valuable insights about yourself and others.

  So, whenever you share something bothering you, do not focus on the judgment you may or may not receive. Focus on how that act will help you leave narcissism behind, find new ways to address the issue and become more connected to others, leading to growth and a better life.

- **Surround Yourself with Supportive People:** We all need someone we can turn to with our vulnerabilities. Therefore, build and maintain a network of individuals who appreciate and respect your vulnerability. Their support can boost your confidence and make it easier to open up.

Seek out family members, friends, or colleagues who are empathetic and understanding, share your experiences with them, and notice how their positive responses help alleviate your fear of judgment. Being around supportive people creates a safe space to express your true self. This network provides emotional support and reinforces the idea that vulnerability is a natural and valuable aspect of human connection.

How to Include Vulnerability in Daily Life

Step 1: Start Small: You do not have to share what you are not comfortable sharing. Just begin practicing vulnerability with small acts, like sharing a personal story or admitting you don't know something. These small steps will help you get used to being honest about your feelings, experiences, and thoughts.

Gradually, as you gain confidence and experience the benefits of vulnerability, you can build up to sharing more significant experiences. Starting small will make the process more manageable and less overwhelming.

Step 2: Reflect on Your Experiences: At the end of the day, take time to reflect on the experiences from the different situations or circumstances where you were vulnerable. What did you learn? How did it feel? Who understands you better?

This practice helps you become more comfortable with vulnerability over time. When you analyze your feelings, thoughts, and the outcomes from the experience, you can better understand the benefits of being open and develop a more positive attitude towards vulnerability.

Step 3: Celebrate Your Courage: All the strategies for overcoming narcissism require some level of bravery, including being vulnerable. Therefore, celebrate all the steps you take to show vulnerability (small and big).

Recognizing and celebrating your efforts, steps, and wins highlights the positive aspects of vulnerability and can boost your confidence and encourage you to continue embracing vulnerability. This, in turn, helps build a habit of openness and self-compassion.

Worksheet:

Action 1: Fear Identification Exercise:

Exercise: Write down at least three fears that prevent you from being open and authentic with others. Reflect on where these fears originate and how they have influenced your behavior and relationships. Challenge yourself to confront these fears by sharing with a trusted friend or journaling about how they have held you back.

_____

_____

_____

_____

_____

_____

_____

_____

_____

_____

_____

_____

Action 2: Vulnerability Timeline:

Exercise: Write about moments when vulnerability played a significant role. Include both positive and negative experiences where opening up had an impact on you. Think of how such experiences helped shape your understanding of vulnerability and influenced your relationships. Share one of these moments with someone close to you to deepen your connection and practice vulnerability.

_____

_____

_____

_____

_____

_____

_____

_____

_____

_____

_____

Action 3: Daily Vulnerability Challenge:

Exercise: Start by setting a small goal to practice vulnerability, such as expressing a personal preference to a friend or admitting a mistake at work. Reflect on how it felt to be open and whether it brought you closer to the person you shared with. Try a more significant goal after a week of practicing with small vulnerability goals.

Action 4: Celebrating Vulnerability:

Exercise: At the end of each week, take time to celebrate your moments of vulnerability. Write down the positive effects or lessons learned from sharing your experiences or feelings with others. Acknowledge your courage and progress in embracing vulnerability as a strength rather than a weakness. Also, talk to someone about your reflections to reinforce the positive impact of being open.

_____

_____

_____

_____

_____

_____

_____

_____

Action 5: Practice Mindful Vulnerability:

Exercise: Before sharing something personal or expressing a vulnerable emotion, take a moment to center yourself and observe any anxieties or fears that arise. Use deep breathing or grounding techniques to calm your body and mind. Notice how mindfulness enhances your ability to be present and exercise vulnerability.

From this chapter, you have come to realize that the vulnerability you thought was a weakness is a helpful quality you must embrace. Follow the tips, strategies, and steps provided to learn how to become vulnerable and reap all the benefits, including overcoming narcissism.

Let's get to chapter 12, our last chapter, which covers seeking professional help as a way to stop being a narcissist and live an authentic life.

Chapter 12: Seeking Professional Help

Even though one cannot be medically diagnosed with NPD until they are 18 years old, for most of us, we learn these traits from a very young age. It is the only way of living we've known only that now, we are grown and know better and have the power and resources to change the narrative. However, the wound is likely deeply rooted in our psychological makeup, making it challenging to address without expert guidance.

And,

Even though <u>only 6% percent of us have been diagnosed with NPD</u>, you wouldn't really rule out this mental condition (or work on it) without the evaluation and guidance of a professional.

That is why seeking professional help is another strategy you must include in this journey. Therapy can provide personalized strategies and support to help you understand and modify these behaviors. This chapter will explore the benefits of seeking professional help, how to find the best therapist to work with, and how to make the most of therapy to foster lasting change.

Let's get started!

Understanding the Need for Professional Help

Working on your own to overcome something as complex as narcissism or NPD can be challenging. You are trying to change what you know and convince your brain that the change that's happening is good. As we said, the subconscious mind doesn't like change. Therefore, the whole experience of unlearning the old traits and learning new ones can be overwhelming, and without guidance, you might easily find yourself running back to the comfort of your narcissist traits.

On the other hand, including a therapist in this journey will provide an objective and supportive environment where you can explore and understand your specific underlying issues. Your therapist will walk with you throughout your journey, from uncovering the root causes of your narcissistic tendencies to guiding you through the process of change using techniques that best find your unique personality.

If you want to achieve lasting personal growth, you need not just to be open to seeking professional help but to actualize it, too.

How?

First, you need to find a therapist, and not just any therapist. You need a therapist who understands your needs, has a good reputation, and is experienced so your journey becomes easier and successful.

Let's find out how to do that.

Finding the Right Therapist

There are different types of therapists, but for you to have an effective experience, look for licensed professionals who specialize in personality disorders or have specific training in narcissistic traits.

And where can you get them?

First, you can ask for **recommendations** from trusted sources, such as healthcare providers, friends, or family. Secondly, you can look **online**; all you need to do is google "Where to get a therapist who specializes in personality disorder near me," and different websites will provide you with different leads. You will find leads to both in-person and virtual therapists. However, do your due diligence from professional directories, online reviews, or by interacting with them on their social media pages or websites to gain insights into their qualifications and approach.

Ensure that you feel comfortable and understood by the therapist you choose. During your first consultation, have a list of things you need to know, understand, and communicate, from session schedule and fees to your goals and concerns, to determine if the therapist's style, expertise, and charges align with your needs. And even with everything put into consideration, the bottom line is that the right therapist should ***create a safe, non-judgmental space*** where you can openly explore your thoughts and behaviors.

This step may take time, but the effort will bear effective, long-term transformation.

Moving on, let's discuss the different types of therapy to help you choose the best therapist to work with.

Types of Therapy

There are several therapeutic approaches for addressing narcissistic behaviors, but here are the three main ones to choose from:

1) *Cognitive Behavioral Therapy (CBT)*

A therapist who uses the CBT[33] approach aims to help you identify and change distorted thinking patterns and behaviors. This method focuses on developing healthier thought processes and coping mechanisms and is more effective in addressing the core cognitive distortions associated with narcissistic behaviors, such as entitlement and a need for constant admiration.

Challenging negative beliefs and attitudes encourages you to adopt a rational, more balanced, healthier, and constructive way of thinking. Through regular sessions and homework assignments, CBT will help you build new, healthier habits and responses to situations that previously triggered narcissistic reactions.

---

[33] https://www.researchgate.net/profile/Alexis-Matusiewicz?_tp=eyJjb250ZXh0Ijp7ImZpcnN0UGFnZSI6InB1YmxpY2F0aW9uIiwicGFnZSI6InB1YmxpY2F0aW9uIn19

2) *Dialectical Behavior Therapy (DBT)*

With <u>Dialectical Behavior Therapy</u>[34], the focus will be on managing intense emotions and improving relationships through skills like emotional regulation, effective communication, and mindfulness. This type of therapy combines cognitive-behavioral techniques with concepts from Eastern mindfulness practices, providing tools to handle anger, stress, and interpersonal conflicts more effectively.

If you go for this approach, you will participate in individual therapy and skills training groups, which will help reduce impulsive behaviors and enhance empathy towards others. You will learn to balance acceptance and change, nurturing emotional stability and healthier interactions.

---

[34] <u>https://www.grouporttherapy.com/blog/dialectical-behavior-therapy-narcissistic-personality-disorder#:~:text=DBT%20can%20help%20individuals%20with%20NPD%20develop%20more%20effective%20communication,who%20struggle%20with%20self-awareness</u>.

3) *Psychodynamic Therapy*: *Transference Focused Psychotherapy (TFP)*

The third approach involves addressing the issue from the root cause by <u>exploring the unconscious motivations</u>[35] (thoughts and beliefs) behind your behaviors and helping you understand how past experiences influence your current actions.

Here, your therapist will help you delve into your early childhood experiences and unresolved conflicts, among other factors that contribute to narcissist traits, providing insights on what you need to address and how best to do it.

With someone to show you how, you will learn emotional intelligence and self-awareness, qualities that we have seen help you recognize and address narcissistic behaviors. Through your sessions, you will develop a habit of interpreting, understanding, and reframing your thoughts, feelings, and behaviors, leading to effective and lasting personal change.

---

[35]

https://www.researchgate.net/publication/235336688_Psychodynamic_Psychotherapy_for_Narcissistic_Personality

Now that you have decided on the therapist to walk with in this journey and the best approach that fits your needs and areas of concern, let's find out what you should expect from your first session to the last.

What to Expect from The Process of Therapy

Even though different professionals use different approaches and styles, therapy involves a collaborative process that involves regular sessions and active participation, and here's what to expect from it:

- **Assessment**

During the first few sessions, your therapist will conduct an assessment to understand your history, behaviors, and goals. Here, expect interviews and possibly questionnaires to help your therapist gather comprehensive information about your symptoms, background, and current emotional and psychological state.

This will help them identify specific narcissistic traits and other primary issues, which will help them create a tailored treatment plan. This initial phase is important as it sets a clear direction for therapy and ensures the interventions are appropriate for your needs.

- **Goal Setting**

From the assessment, together with your therapist, you will create realistic and achievable goals aimed at addressing your specific narcissist traits. These goals might include developing empathy, improving relationships, adopting a positive mindset, developing self-compassion, or managing narcissistic tendencies such as defensiveness, blame game, and the need for external validation.

With clear and specific goals for your aspirations and therapeutic objectives (to learn ways to overcome narcissistic traits), you will have a roadmap to help you stay focused and motivated.

Note: You will regularly revisit and adjust these goals to ensure they remain relevant and attainable as you progress.

- **Skill Development**

During this stage of your therapy process, your therapist will introduce practical tools that will help you develop specific skills to address narcissistic behaviors. It could be improving communication skills, managing emotions effectively, or dealing with self-criticism. Whichever skill you work on during any session will be aimed at changing the dysfunctional narcissistic patterns.

Your therapist might use techniques such as mindfulness exercises, role-playing, and cognitive restructuring to help develop these skills. Ensure to practice and refine these techniques to make your journey successful.

- **Homework and Practice**

After you've learned a new skill or strategy, your therapist will likely assign you homework to practice it in real-life situations. This practice is essential for reinforcing what you learn in therapy. Common therapy homework includes journaling, mindfulness practices, or specific social interactions aimed at applying your new skills.

Ensure you consistently complete your homework to help bridge the gap between therapy sessions and daily life. This will help make the new behaviors habitual, which is crucial for internalizing the changes and making lasting improvements.

- **Progress Evaluation**

From time to time, you will notice that you have sessions where you reflect on and evaluate your progress. Such sessions are essential as they help ensure that your treatment plan is effective and allow you to make adjustments if needed.

During these evaluations, you and your therapist will review your goals, discuss any challenges, and celebrate successes. This ongoing assessment will help you identify any areas where you might need additional support or different strategies.

Regularly evaluating your progress helps ensure your therapy journey stays dynamic, responsive, and helpful, continually adapting to your evolving needs and goals and ensuring sustained change, learning, and growth.

Making the Most of Therapy

To make sure you make the best out of your sessions and actually see improvement:

1) **Stay Committed:** Ensure you show up for your therapy sessions and actively participate in each to build consistency, which helps build momentum in your journey. Even when therapy feels challenging, showing up and fully engaging can help boost your mood and lead to breakthroughs and improvement over time.

2) **Be Honest:** Don't even consider signing up for therapy if you plan on leaving honesty at home or in your car; you won't progress with this process. So, during every session, ensure to openly share your thoughts, feelings, and

experiences with your therapist; remember you are in a safe and non-judgmental space.

Being honest allows your therapist to understand your true self and provide the most accurate guidance. Holding back, hiding important information, or lying will hinder your progress and prevent you from addressing the main issues.

3) **Practice Outside of Sessions:** Apart from your homework, be intentional in applying the skills and strategies learned in therapy to your daily life. Practice is the only secret to adopting new behaviors.

Whether it's practicing open communication, setting healthy boundaries, practicing mindfulness, or other therapeutic tools, regular practice helps reinforce these new healthy habits. It makes them a natural part of your life, replacing the narcissistic, unhealthy habits.

4) **Be Patient:** Change takes time, and setbacks are expected in any journey in life. Therefore, be patient with yourself and stay focused on your long-term goals. Recognize that progress may come in small achievements and milestones and that persistence, even during difficult periods, is essential to achieve your main goal: to become

better and adopt new ways of life that bring growth, fulfillment, and genuine happiness.

5) **Seek and Accept Feedback:** Since your therapist is part of this journey, they will give you feedback on your progress and areas needing more attention. Be open to this feedback and use it constructively to improve. Embrace this input with a willingness to adapt and grow to enhance the **effectiveness of your therapy.**

Worksheet:

Action 1: Therapist Compatibility Checklist:

Exercise: Create a checklist of qualities you seek in a therapist. Keep in mind factors like experience, specialization in personality disorders, and approachability. Rank these qualities from most to least important and use them to evaluate potential therapists.

_____

_____

_____

_____

_____

_____

_____

_____

_____

_____

_____

_____

Action 2: Goal Setting Exercise:

Exercise: Write down the behaviors or thought patterns you want to change. For each goal, outline two actionable steps (from what we have covered) you can take outside of therapy sessions to work towards these changes. Remember to start small.

_____

_____

_____

_____

_____

_____

_____

_____

_____

_____

_____

Action 3: Therapist Interview Preparation:

Exercise: Prepare a list of questions for your initial consultation with a therapist. Remember to include every query, no matter how insignificant it seems.

_____

_____

_____

_____

_____

_____

_____

_____

_____

_____

Action 4: Have Reflection Journal:

Exercise: Have a journal to write your thoughts and emotions before and after therapy sessions. Use this journal to note any insights gained, challenges faced, or progress made. Revisit your journal periodically to identify patterns or areas you need to explore more with your therapist.

Action 5: Develop Skills learned in Therapy:

Exercise: After learning a skill, set aside time each day to engage in activities that reinforce it.

Action 6: Feedback Integration:

Exercise: Request feedback from your therapist after several sessions. Ask about your progress, areas needing improvement, and suggestions for enhancing your therapeutic journey. Reflect on this feedback and absorb it into your ongoing therapy goals and practices.

Sure, there is still some stigma on seeking professional help, but you must embrace this courageous step to overcome narcissistic behaviors. You will receive the tools, support, and guidance needed to foster genuine change. Therefore, do not let anyone convince you that therapy does not work or that it is for a certain group of people. You know what you stand to gain from this journey; make the right decision and experience all the benefits of seeking professional help.

Conclusion

Marthe, a fictional character in Michelle Gable's National Bestseller, *A Paris Apartment*, says something that sums up what you need to do to stop being a narcissist and to stop controlling behavior in relationships. She says:

"Always ask yourself if there is a better way to express your feelings."

So, as you practice all the strategies, tools, tips, and steps we've discussed, internalize this sentiment. It will help you recognize when you are acting narcissistically —or are about to— in your relationships and stop yourself from doing it in favor of a more constructive response.

Good luck!

PS: I'd like your feedback. If you are happy with this book, please leave a review on Amazon.

Please leave a review for this book on Amazon by visiting the page below:

https://amzn.to/2VMR5qr